Story of the Spirit

Story of the Spirit

Knowing Who He Is Transforms Who You Become

SARAH JO FAIRCHILD

Foreword by Todd H. Fetters

RESOURCE *Publications* • Eugene, Oregon

STORY OF THE SPIRIT
Knowing Who He Is Transforms Who You Become

Resource Publications
An Imprint of Wipf and Stock Publishers
199 W. 8th Ave., Suite 3
Eugene, OR 97401

www.wipfandstock.com

PAPERBACK ISBN: 978-1-5326-4405-4
HARDCOVER ISBN: 978-1-5326-4406-1
EBOOK ISBN: 978-1-5326-4407-8

Manufactured in the U.S.A.   08/09/18

For my parents
who first introduced me to God
and continually inspire me to trust Him more.

Contents

Foreword by Todd H. Fetters | ix
Acknowledgments | xi
Introduction: The Trust Connection | xiii

Chapter One
First Impressions: Genesis 1:2 | 1

Chapter Two
Bezalel and the Legacy Builder: Exodus 35–39 | 7

Chapter Three
Moses and the Cultivator of Community:
Numbers 11:1–26 | 16

Chapter Four
Othniel and the Champion of Second Chances:
Judges 3:7–11 | 24

Chapter Five
Gideon and the Author of Impossible Scripts: Judges 6–7 | 31

Chapter Six
Jephthah and the Redeemer of the Rejected:
Judges 11:1–33 | 43

Chapter Seven
Samson and the Just Deliverer: Judges 13–16 | 51

Chapter Eight
Saul and the Source of Peace: 1 Samuel 9–15 | 61

Chapter Nine
David and the Hope of the Fallen:
1 Samuel 16—2 Samuel 23 | 69

Chapter Ten
Elijah and the Mover of Men: 1 Kings 18:1–12 | 77

Chapter Eleven
Prophets, Kings, and the Voice of Truth:
2 Chronicles 15–20 | 85

Chapter Twelve
Mary, Messiah, and the Spring of Life: Luke 1:26–35 | 94

Chapter Thirteen
The Epilogue: 2 Corinthians 5:5–20 | 101

Appendix A
For Use in a Small Group or Sunday School | 105

Appendix B
For Use in a Sermon Series | 107

Bibliography | 109

Foreword

"Come, Holy Spirit."

The time is right for modern Christians to embrace this ancient prayer and recite it regularly; not as a formula, but as an essential breathing rhythm that sustains everyday life.

In the morning, when the day begins with fresh opportunities we can pray, "Come, Holy Spirit."

During the day, as decisions need to be made, or loneliness settles in, when truth needs to be told, or as temptations keep darting by, we can pray, "Come, Holy Spirit."

At the end of the day when peace of mind is desired and rest is required, we can pray, "Come, Holy Spirit."

But when we pray, "Come, Holy Spirit," it is good to know who we are seeking and why his presence matters.

The Christian faith is unapologetically and wonderfully trinitarian. We believe in God the Father, God the Son, and God the Holy Spirit. Each person important. Each person indispensable to the mission of God and the manifestation of Christ's Kingdom. However, we can unwittingly prefer one more than the others. I did. My affinity was toward the Father who created me and the Son who redeemed me. While I believed in the Holy Spirit, sadly my relationship with Him—if one could call it a relationship—mostly engaged my mind. According to John 14:23, however, my relationship with the Triune God becomes a reality as God takes up residence in my heart.

This is where *The Story of the Spirit* can help you. Sarah Fairchild has carefully considered the presence and the work of the Holy Spirit in the lives of ordinary men and women who impacted their community in extraordinary ways. They reveal the remarkable potential of a relational connection with him.

The same can be true of you today.

Your life of extraordinary impact starts with the bold pursuit of knowing the Holy Spirit better and trusting him more. So, before you start to read Sarah's thoughtful book, do something courageous—pray these three words, "Come Holy Spirit."

Rev. Todd H. Fetters
Bishop
Church of the United Brethren in Christ

Acknowledgments

Teddy, my husband and friend, you continue inspiring bravery I never knew I was capable of. Thank you for the encouragement, insights, and support throughout this adventure.

Julz, Gabriel, and Hendrix, you infuse my life with meaning and laughter. I love you so much and pray God's absolute best for the chapters ahead of you. May you grow increasingly aware of the way He adores you and is worthy of your trust.

Bishop Todd H. Fetters, your earnest effort to lead well in the kingdom leaves little room for extra projects like this. Thank you for making time to encourage me and write the foreword for this study.

I would inevitably miss someone if I attempted to list every educator, classmate, mentor, and friend who impacted my life and enriched my journey of leading others in the adventure of knowing God better and trusting him more. He knows the significance of your role in my life. Thank you!

I applaud the publishing team for taking a chance on me and finding value in this fusion of theology swaddled in story. It has been my privilege to research and write the Spirit's story in this way. Thank you for helping make that possible.

Introduction

The Trust Connection

He can recall the accident like it happened yesterday. One second the car was cruising serenely down the highway and the next it was spinning in slow motion circles towards the guardrail. Time stood still as the initial impact seared itself in memory, each scene frozen in snapshot flashes. The shutter clicked to capture shards of splintered glass suspended eerily mid-air. His arms floated upwards on their own accord.

Click.

Then slammed down without warning.

Click-click.

His head snapped to the right with the car's final roll, and a surge of pain exploded down his spine. Darkness danced along the edges of his sight, threatening to engulf his frail hold on consciousness. Blinking back panic, he laid helpless and afraid.

Then someone called his name.

He knew that voice. He struggled to see through pain-laced tears, and for a split-second, a familiar face came into focus. The shutter clicked once more before blurred vision faded to black, but it didn't matter anymore. He wasn't alone anymore. His father was here. Dad was here, and everything was going to be okay.

～

No-one plans for tragedy. It strikes in unexpected ways, forever severing life into before and after sections. The car crash that claims your ability to walk. The cancer diagnosis that derails retirement dreams. The divorce that fractures your family in two.

When our world is spinning out of control, we instinctively reach for someone we can trust. Strangers offer little security, but we find refuge in a familiar voice, a familiar face. We crave that comfort of connection because we're created with a relational blueprint. We want relationships that feel like home, places of safety amidst life's storms. Whether it's the connection between father and son, husband and wife, or lifelong best friends, we want to know and be known, to trust and be trusted. Those are the relationships we can lean on when our world flips upside down and leaves us feeling lost and alone.

It takes time to build bonds strong enough to weather tragedies like the one portrayed above. That's just as true in our relationship with God as it is with our friends and family. Knowing him is more than knowing facts about him. It means connecting with every part of who he is and trusting him wholeheartedly so that in life's darkest moments, the mere sound of his voice floods our soul with waves of peace that surpass understanding.

Since you're holding this book in your hands, I presume you desire a deeper intimacy in your relationship with God. I long for that as well, but until recently I mistakenly limited my connection to two-thirds capacity. This unsettling realization dawned during an otherwise ordinary lecture in seminary. My professor expounded on various doctrines of the Trinity while I hastily scratched down notes until an unexpected rush of emotion interrupted my efforts. Something akin to grief washed over me. The frantic writing ceased, pen poised over paper as the sobering awareness that stung like accusation sunk in.

At that moment I realized my relationship with the Holy Spirit was little more than the scribblings of a graduate student focused on the final exam. Sure, I could quote verses about him and speak in cliché phrases on Spirit-filled living, but I felt little to no real connection with this piece of who God was. I intellectually affirmed his importance while inadvertently treating him like the third wheel of the Trinity.

Conversations with classmates and fellow ministry leaders revealed a similar sense of disconnect. Christians often struggle to relate to the Holy Spirit in the same way we connect with God as our Father or Jesus as our Savior and Friend. Unable to make sense of the mystery masked in confusion and controversy, we settle for less than we long for in our relationship with him. We settle for a two-thirds connection.

If this notion bothers you as much as it did me, then take heart! There is a way to remedy the relational barriers associated with the Spirit. We can uncover who he is and why he matters. It's a journey of discovery that will forever deepen your relationship with this vital member of the Godhead.

So where do we start?

Getting to know someone happens in layers. For example, a dating profile gives you a surface understanding of a person but talking with a friend who knows them in real life adds a richer depth. Eventually, you'll meet them in person, and the initial interest inspired by reading their profile and listening to stories from mutual friends can develop into something more profound. As you interact with them in various settings over time, you witness a consistency in their character and discover who they truly are. That's when trust begins to grow.

Our relationship with the Spirit follows the same pattern. We can access a personal profile of sorts through books categorizing his qualities as revealed in the New Testament. Such volumes serve as valuable resources in getting to know him, but a more vibrant layer of his identity emerges in the Old Testament through the stories of real people who encountered the Spirit in real life.

Experiencing him through their eyes encourages a greater depth of understanding by revealing the consistency of his character among various shades of his personality. They don't just tell us who he is; they show us why he's worth trusting for the unpredictable, unfolding chapters of our own life. Their stories unveil a Spirit who cultivates community, empowers justice, emboldens the insecure, champions second chances, and transforms places of wounding into places of worship. We discover why knowing him makes all the difference amidst the difficulties of leadership, the devastation of loss, and the day-to-day realities of living in a broken world.

We've settled for a two-thirds connection long enough. Let's not waste another day lingering in the shallow end for fear of dredging up controversy or dealing with confusion. It's time to turn the page in our relationship with the Trinity's most mysterious member and dive into the soul-deep connection we crave with the whole of who God is—Father, Son, *and* Spirit.

Chapter One

_____

First Impressions

Genesis 1:2

Darkness wraps the world in isolation. Land lays waste beneath a watery grave, buried in shifting shadows of the deep. Aimless waves churn at the surface, echoing like an eerie lullaby, a restless rhythm ricocheting against the endless void. It is a hauntingly hollow scene without a hint of significance or spectacle, yet this is the unlikely stage upon which the Holy Spirit first moves.

We catch our initial glimpse of him here in this lonely abyss, hovering above the murky waters. His presence ushers in a holy hush, and the primordial sea stills as if waiting for what comes next. As he lingers a growing sense of expectation infuses the empty air with whispers of something fresh, something new, something altogether unknown. From this barren backdrop, the Spirit births life.

> "In the beginning, God created the heavens and the earth. Now the earth was formless and empty, darkness was over the surface of the deep, and the Spirit of God was hovering over the waters" (Gen 1:1–2).

Before God spoke and light pierced blackness, before the waters divided and mountains flowered with forests, before man took his first breath and beheld his Maker, the Spirit hovered. As the curtain rises on creation, Scripture paints this peculiar picture

1

of him, a portrait many find more ominous than inspiring. Such an introduction illustrates the very reason why we wrestle to relate to this part of who God is. From this strange opening scene to later images like the dove at Christ's baptism or tongues of fire at Pentecost, Scripture describes him in disconcerting ways, penning the Spirit's story with a perplexing veil of secrecy.

As noted previously in the introduction, we connect more naturally with God as Father than the mysterious Spirit because we have some sense of how special that parental bond can be. Whether or not we experienced it ourselves, we can envision what that relationship should look like. We know a Dad is supposed to be good. He's supposed to guard us, guide us, and love us as we grow.

God is that goodness perfected. He is the ultimate provider and protector. He inspires his children to be brave, affirms that we are valuable, and fights for us at every turn. Even when we stray, he waits with the light on, arms opened wide to welcome us home. We know we are prized in his eyes through passages like Matthew 6:26. "Look at the birds of the air, that they do not sow, nor reap nor gather into barns, and yet your heavenly Father feeds them. Are you not worth much more than they?"

We also relate to God as the Son who traded in heaven's perfection for flawed humanity. We identify with Jesus as one who knows the thrill of celebration and throb of sorrow, the beauty of love and bitter taste of betrayal. He made himself one of us, God in the flesh living amongst us. "No one has ever seen God, but the one and only Son, who is himself God and is in closest relationship with the Father, has made him known" (John 1:18).

This kinship with Christ brings comfort, and we find courage in our connection with God as Father, but we often stumble when attention shifts to the Trinity's most mysterious member. Wary of wading too deeply into controversial and confusing waters, we keep the Holy Spirit safely at arm's length. We settle for a two-thirds connection and miss out on the broader intimacy we crave.

In 2 Corinthians 13:14 the Apostle Paul writes, "May the grace of the Lord Jesus Christ, and the love of God, and the fellowship of the Holy Spirit be with you all." If we relate to God only as Father and Son, we miss out on this fullness of fellowship. The Spirit is vital for a vibrant relationship with the God who loves us, yet we face real complications in our quest to understand him, beginning with this uncanny first impression.

Sometimes the richest parts of a person require more time and effort to unearth. Certain traits aren't always evident on the surface, but as we clear away the obscurity, we realize the value of those hidden layers. Applying that sentiment to Scripture's introduction of the Spirit will revolutionize the way we understand this passage and reveal a shade of his personality that our hearts, our homes, and our world desperately needs.

Our treasure hunt begins by tracing implications of the original language often lost in translation. Two Hebrew words pair together to describe this opening scene of the Spirit's story where the earth is "formless and empty." The first is *tohuw*, which portrays a wasted space void of purpose or worth. The second term is a synonym, *bohuw*, which conveys a similar sense of hollowness. When spoken together the sound of the Hebrew words themselves delivers a sense of dreariness. *Tohuw bohuw*. One might compare it to the modern phrase, "blah, blah, blah." The earth was *tohuw bohuw*; the earth was blah, blah, blah.

It was nothing.

Until the Spirit entered the scene.

He did not observe from afar, distant and detached. He drew near the watery wasteland, and He lingered. He stayed. He hovered.

The word "hover" is the Hebrew verb, *rachaph*, which means to relax or grow soft. It's also translated as trembling, stirring, or fluttering. When I read the word "hover," I can't help but picture a ghost-like figure floating eerily above the water, but "flutter" prompts an image less unnerving and more enthralling.

It reminds me of a butterfly.

We don't encounter butterflies very often in town, but on the rare occasion one flutters into our yard something unusual happens. Like most little boys, my six-year-old spends his outdoor time kicking balls, swinging bats, and finding random things to throw. He can be thoroughly engrossed in an imaginary battle, defending our home with sticks for swords and sounds effects galore, but if a butterfly enters the scene, my little warrior halts.

He's mesmerized, frozen motionless for one magical moment. Silence settles over the scene. He barely breathes for fear of shattering the sacred moment and scaring the butterfly away. A few heartbeats later the spell is broken, and he's back to tromping, stomping and general six-year-old business, but that instant, that pause in the chaos of play when the sight of a butterfly stills his whole world illustrates the essence of *rachaph*.

This change in imagery reveals a striking contrast between the bleakness of the waters and the captivating presence of the Spirit. Curiously enough this literary contrast appears only one other place in Scripture. It surfaces here in the beginning of Genesis and again at the end of Deuteronomy, the bookends of a section of Scripture referred to as the Torah or Pentateuch.

Perhaps it is coincidental that the only two places in Scripture contrasting *tohuw* with *rachaph* occur at the opening and closing of this sacred collection of books, but that seems unlikely. Rather, the significance of these two Spirit-centered references sandwiching the Torah's foundational teachings asserts his intimate involvement with God's work in this world. This second reference appears in a poetic reflection of Israel's history composed by Moses shortly before his death, a song recounting God's faithfulness to his chosen people.

> "For the Lord's portion is his people, Jacob his allotted inheritance. In a desert land, he found him, in a barren and howling waste. He shielded him and cared for him; he guarded him as the apple of his eye, like an eagle that stirs up its nest and hovers over its young, that spreads its wings to catch them and carries them aloft" (Deut 32:9–11).

The Spirit's hovering presence preceded the world's first flash of light. Here, the same Hebrew terms portray his partnership in the formation of a people chosen to shine among the nations. Both instances reveal his illuminating nature. He sees potential in

4

the darkness, and where others see waste, he envisions unlikely possibilities.

First, he fluttered into the shadowy void. He was the quiet pause before the fireworks of creation, the stillness before the world exploded in fresh life. Then he helped fashion an entire nation from the once-barren womb of Abraham's wife, Sarah. He stayed present with Israel like an eagle watching over her young. Of all the canvases God could have chosen to create this world from, of all the wombs he could have chosen to birth his people from, the Spirit chose the unlikely, the unlovely, the impossible.

That is a Spirit worth knowing. That is a Spirit we need more of. There is no place, no person beyond his reach. He is the one who forms worth from waste and fashions beauty from barrenness.

Our world is not the paradise God intended. We face days when chaos crowds in and our soul desperately needs a moment of stillness. We face wilderness seasons when life stretches out before us like an endless, dreary desert. The Spirit meets us there. He invades the emptiness. He doesn't pass over us; he draws near instead. He enters the scene, makes himself part of our story, and ushers in a moment that's a little bit magical.

The ghostly image of an unknowable, unrelatable, hovering Spirit no longer fits. Our first introduction to him, now rightly understood, reveals a person we're inspired to know better and trust more. I welcome His presence in the darkest corners of my heart. I want him to illuminate potential within me I never imagined possible. Our families, our churches, our world needs a fresh infusion of Spirit-fueled life, and it begins by embracing this first piece of who he is and why he matters.

What a wonderful revelation.

What an inspiring invitation.

And to think, this is only our first impression!

DIGGING DEEPER:

- In what ways have other people recognized or suggested "untapped potential" in your life?

- How did you feel about their observation?

- Read Psalms 139:1–16. What does this passage teach you about the Spirit who knows every delightful and dysfunctional detail about you?

- "Of all the canvases God could have chosen to create this world from, of all the wombs he could have chosen to birth his people from, the Spirit chose the unlikely, the unlovely, the impossible." What area of your life could benefit from a closer connection with this kind of Spirit?

- Grab a sheet of paper and draw three boxes. Sketch an image that portrays God as Father in the first box. Draw a picture that expresses who Jesus is in the second box and who the Spirit is in the third. Which "snapshot" was easiest, and why do you suppose that is?

- We often see Spirit-filled living in the context of something we do rather than someone we know. What barriers have you encountered in connecting with the Spirit as a Person you can know? How does this relate to the "trust connection" addressed in the Introduction?

Chapter Two

Bezalel and the Legacy Builder

Exodus 35–39

My youngest has the recipe for box brownies memorized. It's a family favorite for carry-ins, class parties, and random rainy days in need of chocolate. He enjoys cracking the eggs into the bowl and "stabbing" the yolks. Apparently, that's the way boys make brownies: one-part charming chef, two-parts sword-wielding warrior! He knows it takes a hearty whisking to mix the eggs with the oil and water because the latter ingredients don't play well together. You can dump them into the same bowl, but they never fully dissolve into one another.

Oil and water are essential for tasty brownies, but they also serve up a pretty sweet spiritual illustration. In the last chapter we discovered the Spirit's ability to recognize potential in forgotten places and fashion worth from waste. After such an impactful first impression, it's surprising to note his sudden disappearance from Scripture's narrative.

The Old Testament timeline moves forward as faithful heroes like Abraham, Isaac, and Jacob enter the story, but the Spirit remains silent. Israel explodes into a nation of substance and encounters unjust enslavement by order of an intimidated Pharaoh, but still the Spirit stays silent. Oppression worsens. Israel weeps.

God responds by launching a miraculous rescue mission, all without explicit mention of the Spirit.

Scripture doesn't offer a specific explanation, but let me suggest a one-part Bible, two-parts brownie inspired insight. Oil and water don't mix; neither do sin and the Spirit. Within the first few chapters of Genesis, sin infected the world, crippling creation and corrupting humankind.

> "The Lord saw how great the wickedness of the human race had become on the earth, and that every inclination of the thoughts of the human heart was only evil all the time. The Lord regretted that he had made human beings on the earth, and his heart was deeply troubled" (Gen 6:5–6).

If you backtrack a few verses earlier you'll notice this phrase: "My Spirit will not contend with man forever" (v 3). The one powerful enough to transform a watery wasteland into paradise will not reside where sin reigns. Just like oil and water, sin and the Spirit cannot occupy the same space.

> "For the flesh desires what is contrary to the Spirit, and the Spirit what is contrary to the flesh. They are in conflict with each other" (Gal 5:17).

When humankind rebelled against God, they quenched the Spirit, but after centuries of sin-induced silence, he re-enters the storyline at a pivotal point in Israel's formation. Just as his hovering presence preceded the stirring of something new at creation, so it marks a fresh beginning for Israel. On the first day of the third month following their radical redemption from Egyptian slavery, God speaks to his people. He reveals his plan for a prosperous future contingent only upon their faithfulness.

> "You yourselves have seen what I did to Egypt, and how I carried you on eagles' wings and brought you to myself. Now if you obey me fully and keep my covenant, then out of all nations, you will be my treasured possession. Although the whole earth is mine, you will be for me a kingdom of priests and a holy nation" (Exod 19:4–6).

God offers the newly liberated people the promise of a covenant. Upon their wholehearted acceptance, he announces his intentions to build a sanctuary among them, a tabernacle he will fill with his presence. For the first time since the garden where perfection fell into peril and sin stained the hearts of humanity, God planned to dwell among his people again. The tent-like sanctuary signified the restored relationship and covenant commitment between Creator and creation. Who better to coordinate such a significant endeavor than the Spirit who stirred life from barrenness in the very beginning?

The splendor of the structure would reflect the reality it symbolized, the wonder of God's presence amidst the Israelite people. Exodus 36–39 describes the tabernacle's beauty in stunning detail from intricate carvings of gold and bronze to colorfully woven tapestries and ornate woodworking. The construction of such architectural artistry called for an exceptionally skilled set of hands, and the Spirit who helped fashion Eden's paradise partnered with a builder named Bezalel to create a second dwelling place for God on Earth.

> "The Lord has chosen Bezalel, son of Uri, the son of Hur, of the tribe of Judah, and he has filled him with the Spirit of God, with wisdom, with understanding, with knowledge and with all kinds of skills— to make artistic designs for work in gold, silver and bronze, to cut and set stones, to work in wood and to engage in all kinds of artistic crafts" (Exod 35:30–33).

Typical Sunday school stories center on well-known heroes like Abraham or Joseph, but the Holy Spirit shows up for the second time in human history through a man most of us never hear about. The Bible shares very few details about Bezalel, but we know from this passage that he was the son of Uri, the son of Hur, of the tribe of Judah. In Exodus 17:8–16 we learn that his grandfather, Hur, supported Moses during one of Israel's more infamous battles. As long as Moses kept his arms uplifted towards heaven, God promised Israel the victory. When he grew too weary to raise his arms any longer, Hur stepped in and held up Moses' arms for him. He demonstrated profound courage and perseverance that day, qualities that left quite an impression on his grandson.

Bezalel's appointment honored this godly heritage, but creating the dwelling place for God Almighty was a daunting responsibility. Imagine the risk involved if things went wrong. What if Israel resisted offering such costly materials from their own limited supplies? What if too few laborers joined the workforce? What if Bezalel's leadership fell short and the project suffered? We don't know if Bezalel wrestled with such qualms or if he tackled the work with complete confidence in his calling, but we do know his bravery in partnering with the Spirit built a legacy that outlasted his lifetime.

God provided Bezalel with a helpmate to assist him, a man named Oholiab. No two men were better suited to carry out God's designs for the tabernacle than the two whose very names so perfectly captured the project's purpose. Bezalel's Hebrew name meant "in the shadow of God's protection," while Oholiab's name translated as "tent of the father" or "my father is my tent."[1] Together this dynamic duo oversaw the development of God's dwelling place, a tent-like structure signifying his protective presence among the Israelite people.

Not only did God encourage Bezalel with the support of a partner, but the Spirit ensured he was mentally equipped for the monumental task as well. As we read in Exodus 31:1–3 and again in 35:30–31, the Spirit filled Bezalel with wisdom, understanding, and knowledge. Interestingly enough, we see this same triad elsewhere in Scripture referencing the scene in which the Spirit first revealed himself. "By wisdom, the Lord laid the earth's foundations, by understanding he set the heavens in place; by his knowledge, the watery depths were divided, and the clouds let drop the dew" (Prov 3:19–20).

This throwback to creation reminds us why treasure hunting in Scripture is such an adventure! The continuity in God's Word is no coincidence. The same Spirit active in Earth's beginnings and the formation of a garden where God could walk and talk with his

---

1. Kaiser, *The Expositor's Bible Commentary*, 475.

people now weaves wisdom, understanding, and knowledge together in the building of the tabernacle, a place where Israel could reconnect with the one who fashioned them for relationship.

Distinguishing between these traits enables a fuller appreciation of the Spirit's empowerment of Bezalel for the task ahead of him. The first term of the triad, wisdom, is translated from the Hebrew word *chokmah*. It is an educated discipline applied to various abilities including tailoring, cloth making, carpentry, waging war, navigation at sea, and political administration.[2] It implies that a person of wisdom is a student of his or her own gifting.[3]

It's a common belief among educators that a student truly grasps an idea when they can teach it to someone else. The *Theological Dictionary of the Old Testament* highlights this aspect of *chokmah* with the example of how one might explain medical symptoms and treatments.[4] I recently accompanied a friend to an appointment regarding a serious health scare, and I did my best to listen with a level head and process the information shared. After an hour of circular conversation with the doctor that never quite answered our questions, however, we left with brains that felt like mush. You've probably encountered a similar scenario and can relate to this mingling of fear and frustration. We needed the information that the doctor possessed but felt confused by his continual use of technical terms that meant nothing to us.

Since my brother works in the medical field as a surgical nurse, we talked with him afterwards. Although the doctor's education and experience surpassed his, my brother was able to do what the doctor could not. It only took him a few minutes to explain the medical information in a way that made sense to us. That is *chokmah*. It's more than intellect; it is the ability to translate one's own brilliance into lightbulb moments for others. As the one leading a host of Israelite craftsmen in combined efforts to accomplish such a massive assignment, Bezalel needed this level of wisdom. He would not have enough time to complete every piece of the

2. Exod 28:3, 35:26, 31:1–5; Isa 10:13; Ps107:27; Deut 34:9

3. Sheppard, *International Standard Bible Encyclopedia*, 1082.

4 Muller, *TDOT*, 365.

structure on his own; he needed to teach others how to handle individual tasks so that he was free to guide the overall process.

The Spirit also filled Bezalel with understanding and knowledge. Knowledge is translated from the term *yada* which conveys an awareness that comes from seeing; it's information learned through observation.[5] The Hebrew term *tabuwn* refers to the application of knowledge which we call understanding. It is awareness that manifests itself in action.[6] Bezalel's knowledge of what to do and how to do it only benefitted the project if he put that information into motion, and he trusted the Spirit to help him do just that.

Several chapters worth of design details in Exodus reflect the extent of the task before him. Bezalel oversaw everything from the structural supports, outer curtains, and tent poles to internal items like the ark of hammered gold adorned with cherubim sculptures, the table of acacia wood, the lampstand with flowerlike cups, buds, and blossoms, the altar of incense, the incense perfume itself, the altar of burnt offering, and the basin for washing. Additional instructions accompanied items for priestly use including several garments, an engraved ephod of gold with mounted onyx stones, and a breastplate inlaid with precious gems like turquoise, emerald, and amethyst.

The Bible describes Bezalel as a gifted artist, but the tremendous task of completing such a wide variety of items demanded far more than one craftsman's creative skills. It required the ability to bring others into the vision God designed, guiding the group to work together towards their common goal. It meant navigating interpersonal dynamics among laborers in addition to the duty of construction itself. The assignment necessitated more than natural aptitude, so the Spirit infused Bezalel's limited skill with his infinite insight and supplied all the wisdom, understanding and knowledge necessary to fulfill the commissioning.

Through his partnership with Bezalel, we discover the Spirit's penchant for building beautiful things. In the beginning, he helped

5. Henry and R.K.H., *International Standard Bible Encyclopedia*, 48.
6. Blomber, *International Standard Bible Encyclopedia*, 945.

fashion the heavens and the earth. From Amazon jungles explod-ing with color to imaginative creatures of the sea, from natural wonders like the Grand Canyon and Victoria Falls to the simple beauty of everyday sunsets, this world exudes his creative genius. Here in Exodus, we see that passion expressed in a skillfully crafted sanctuary symbolizing God's presence among His people. From the lampstand of pure gold engraved with budding leaves and deli-cate almond flowers to finely woven fabrics dyed in majestic jewel tones, the tabernacle rivaled creation's splendor.

Bezalel's story not only reveals the Spirit as an architect of beautiful things, but a builder of beautiful legacies. In 2 Chronicles 1:5, centuries after completion of the tabernacle, the Israelites still referred to the altar as that which Bezalel built. His willingness to embrace an unexpected role in Israel's storyline resulted in a legacy that extended beyond his lifetime. We're offered the same invitation. The Spirit wants to build something beautiful with our life, too.

"You also, like living stones, are being built into a spiritual house to be a holy priesthood, offering spiritual sacrifices acceptable to God through Jesus Christ" (1 Pet 2:5).

"You are no longer foreigners and strangers, but fellow citizens with God's people and also members of his household, built on the foundation of the apostles and prophets, with Christ Jesus himself as the chief corner-stone. In him the whole building is joined together and rises to become a holy temple in the Lord. And in him you too are being built together to become a dwelling in which God lives by his Spirit" (Eph 2:19–22).

The Spirit empowered Bezalel for the creation of his sanctu-ary, a symbol of God's proximity among a unified people of God. Today we no longer worship at that tabernacle because we *are* the tabernacle. For better or worse, God chose to build his kingdom through us. Like the Old Testament sanctuary, we reflect the beau-ty of his presence. We show off his splendor by the way we live and love as one body of believers.

The Spirit encourages us to embrace our calling and shine like stars so that others will see a difference in our actions and feel drawn to God through us (Phil 2:15). He desires that every person experiences the peace and purpose we do as his dearly loved children. We may feel inadequate for such a role, but the Spirit is not. He stands ready and willing to supply what we lack.

Bezalel's story highlights the Spirit's relational heartbeat. Rather than complete the tabernacle on his own—though he was certainly capable of doing so—the Spirit chose to work in partnership with Bezalel. Even the purpose of the project itself emphasizes his desire to cultivate a sense of connectedness. The tabernacle drew Israelites together in shared worship. It unified them as a community identified by the God who once again resided among them. The legacy he built through Bezalel profoundly impacted the whole nation.

That's the kind of legacy I want to leave behind. I want my days on Earth to matter for eternity. I want the Spirit to build something purposeful with my life, something that draws others towards the light of God's love for generations to come. On my own such a feat is laughably impossible! In partnership with the Spirit, however, I have access to all the wisdom, knowledge, and understanding necessary to fulfill my role in furthering the work of the kingdom. I can depend on the Spirit who longs to fashion holy heritages among his people, not ones made of earthly materials but those rich in heavenly treasure. And so can you. We can trust the Builder of beautiful legacies.

DIGGING DEEPER:

- "Like oil and water, sin and the Spirit do not mix." How might the presence of sin—an attitude, habit, or relationship that's pulling you away from the light and towards the shadows—work against your desire to connect with God in a deeper way through this study?

- Take a moment and pray through the following Psalm: *"Search me, God, and know my heart; test me and know my anxious thoughts. See if there is any offensive way in me, and lead me in the way everlasting"* (139:23–24).

- "We may feel inadequate for such a role, but the Spirit is not. He stands ready and willing to supply what we lack." How might your life look differently if you truly embraced this reality?

- What might hold you back?

- How can you address those potential obstacles?

- This chapter revealed the Spirit as a Builder of legacies. How does knowing this aspect of his personality encourage you to trust him more? And how might that trust transform your life?

Chapter Three

Moses and the Cultivator of Community

Numbers 11:1–26

I run now. Slowly. Very slowly. I've crossed the finish line of several races and a handful of half-marathons with just enough energy to stay upright until the end. In case you assume I'm exaggerating to feign humility, let me confess that my goal for a recent race was simply to beat the woman who showed up at the starting line pushing a double stroller. Long story short, I no longer underestimate mothers who tackle races with enough confidence to haul the extra weight of two toddlers up and down the hills! Impressive. Very impressive.

Since I obviously struggle with the sport, you may wonder why I stick with running. I'm not entirely sure myself, but I do know that for a lot of years I let the potential embarrassment of failing keep me from even trying. Now, for the first time, I'm tackling something I'm not sure I'll succeed in. It's terrifying, but the satisfaction of staring fear in the face and finishing despite the battle feels incredible.

I'm not the only one who wrestles with the human habit of avoiding failure. It plagued more than a few favorite heroes of the faith. Take Moses for example. When he first heard God's call from a burning bush to lead the nation of Israel out of Egyptian slavery, his instinctual response dripped with fear. Moses measured himself against the task and came up short. His question in Exodus 3:11 reflects his anxiety: "Who am I that I should go to Pharaoh and bring the Israelites out of Egypt?"

Conflicted with self-doubt, he argued with God Almighty, and the Lord responded to his insecurity with the reassuring reality of his presence. Moses would not face Pharaoh alone. The I AM would lead the way.

Fast forward a few years later, and Moses faced another challenge. As the Israelites' memory of their miraculous rescue faded in the fatigue of wilderness living, they began to complain. And complain. And complain some more. Their persistent pessimism took a toll on Moses. The exhausting efforts of leading a stubborn and ungrateful people pushed him beyond his limits. In running terms, his legs were shot, and no amount of sports drink was going to fuel him to the finish line.

We pick up the story in Numbers 11:14–15. Depleted, defeated, and utterly drained, Moses falls to his knees before God declaring, "I cannot carry all these people by myself; the burden is too heavy for me. If this is how you are going to treat me, please go ahead and kill me—if I have found favor in our eyes—and do not let me face my own ruin."

Running reveals my fear of failure, but it doesn't begin to compare to the depth of depression where death is preferable to facing reality. Most of us can only imagine such a place of soul-draining despair, but some people know exactly how that feels. The couple kneeling beside a tiny grave where they've just buried nine months of hopes and dreams knows that feeling. The betrayed spouse struggling to sort through shards of a shattered marriage can relate. The patient staggering away from a routine physical under the weight of an unexpected diagnosis understands.

Some of us will face realities darker than we ever dreamed possible, but even the blackest nightmare is no match for the I AM. As cliché as it sounds, God is bigger than this world's worst. He beckons his children to relinquish such burdens into his capable hands.

That's exactly what Moses did.

And God answered.

With the Spirit.

God responded to the raw honesty of Moses' plea with reminders of his presence. Despite the messiness of the moment, the Spirit draws near, meeting him in the midst of stormy emotions and churning desperation. He enters the scene to refresh the beaten-down leader and reassure him that he is not alone.

> "The Lord said to Moses: 'Bring me seventy of Israel's elders who are known to you as leaders and officials among the people. Have them come to the tent of meeting, that they may stand there with you. I will come down and speak with you there, and I will take some of the power of the Spirit that is on you and put it on them. They will share the burden of the people with you so that you will not have to carry it alone'" (Num 11:16–17).

It takes courage to start a race you're unsure you can finish but to endure past the breaking point of exhaustion requires more than brave emotion; it demands a commitment more profound than our feelings, a perseverance deeper than the pain. Pushing forward in such an intense state can breed a sense of isolation, and Moses felt utterly alone. He wanted to quit. He longed to die, but the Spirit, a cultivator of community, rallied a team to aid and assist him.

Even with the promise of help, Moses probably wrestled with the prospect of remaining in the position that wearied him to the point of wishing for death. I imagine the temptation to reject God's proposal and resign from leadership anyways nibbled at his mind. Who could fault his aversion to the arduous notion of another lap in the same grueling race that crippled and nearly killed him? After all, leadership transitions are tough, and the last thing Moses needed was a newly assembled crew of leaders potentially complicating an already strenuous situation.

Despite lingering resistance, understandable reservations, and the gravity of his emotionally exhausted state, Moses trusted the sufficiency of the Spirit. He chose to obey. He gathered the elected elders just as God directed, and the community crowded around the tent in eager expectation.

> "Then the Lord came down in the cloud and spoke with him, and he took some of the power of the Spirit that was on him and put it on the seventy elders. When the Spirit rested on them, they prophesied—but did not do so again. However, two men, whose names were Eldad and Medad, had remained in the camp. They were listed among the elders but did not go out to the tent. Yet the Spirit also rested on them, and they prophesied in the camp" (Num 11:25–26).

God proved faithful to his Word. Never before had such a scene played out in Israel's history. For the first time in Scripture, spontaneous prophetic speaking stole over the group, startling all who witnessed the phenomenon. There was nothing subtle about the Spirit's partnership with these seventy elders. He didn't slip quietly into the scene; He stole the show. The surprising spectacle of his presence spotlighted God's appointment of these men and authorized a crucial shift in Israel's leadership structure.

Before we press forward in this encounter between the Spirit, Moses, and the seventy elders, it's important to understand how we should interpret the potentially divisive subject of prophecy. Between a history littered with conflict and lingering confusion in the present, prophecy is somewhat of a loaded term in today's Christian world. While some may find this mystical element of the Holy Spirit's personality enticing, others struggle to relate and shy away. They've seen it misused in ways that dance dangerously close to heresy or reduced to superficial hype.

Prophetic speaking a sensitive issue, but whether or not we feel comfortable with it, whether or not we can wrap our mind around it, prophecy *is* part of the Spirit's story. It's part of who he is. If we crave a deeper connection with the fullness of the Godhead, we must bring this piece of his personality out from the mysterious shadows and into the light.

It may help us understand the Spirit's purpose in such a unique expression of his presence by comparing the scene described among the seventy elders with one that unfolded centuries later at Pentecost. You're probably familiar with the story. After enduring the emotional saga of Christ's journey from the cross to the grave to heaven, the disciples waited to see what might happen next. A veil of uncertainty obscured their vision of the future, but they chose to trust God and bunkered down together just as Jesus instructed. That's when the Spirit revealed himself in an unexpected way.

> "All of them were filled with the Holy Spirit and began to speak in other tongues as the Spirit enabled them. Now there were staying in Jerusalem God-fearing Jews from every nation under heaven. When they heard this sound, a crowd came together in bewilderment, because each one heard their own language being spoken. Utterly amazed, they asked: 'Aren't all these who are speaking Galileans? Then how is it that each of us hears them in our native language? Parthians, Medes and Elamites; residents of Mesopotamia, Judea and Cappadocia, Pontus and Asia, Phrygia and Pamphylia, Egypt and the parts of Libya near Cyrene; visitors from Rome (both Jews and converts to Judaism); Cretans and Arabs—we hear them declaring the wonders of God in our own tongues!' Amazed and perplexed, they asked one another, 'What does this mean?'" (Acts 2:4–12).

In the midst of a tumultuous time for the tiny band of believers, the Spirit reveals his presence with an undeniable display of supernatural power. Imagine the disciples' joy! Jesus was no longer with them, but he did not abandon them. Just as promised, the Spirit arrived, and his presence proved as powerful now as when Christ walked among them in visible form.

A quick comparison between the two instances of mass prophetic speaking offers three essential insights. First, these occurrences were uncommon. It was not part of a religious routine, and we perceive the rarity in the reactions of startled bystanders. Secondly, they marked critical moments in the Spirit's participation with humanity. He does not haphazardly reveal himself in this manner to cause meaningless confusion or chaos. He acts intentionally for a specific purpose. These two points alone preclude the stereotypical images that often come to mind at the mention of prophetic speaking!

Thirdly, and most importantly, they reveal his nature as a cultivator of community. In both instances, the Spirit drew people together in powerful ways. His presence at Pentecost marked the birth of the church and inclusion of individuals from all languages into the one people of God. In the story of Moses and the seventy elders, the prophetic moment marked a significant shift in leadership and validated the authority of those chosen to work alongside Moses.

God forbid we miss out on the extraordinary reality of who the Spirit is because we're too busy arguing over our interpretation of how he shows up! Yes, he conveyed his presence by a flood of prophetic speaking. Yes, that makes some of us squirm in our seats, but if we skip over this interaction to avoid discomfort, we miss the way it highlights his heart for fellowship, for kinship, for community. The Spirit did not leave Moses alone; he answered the wearied leader's pleas for relief by partnering with others to help shoulder the weight.

Today's leaders face equally exhausting realities. Like Moses, they compare themselves with the task at hand and feel inadequate, overburdened, and alone. Sometimes very, very alone. This scene of the Spirit's story reassures us that nothing could be further from the truth. He is with us. His presence is power, and he connects us with others so we can stand firm in him together.

The Spirit's story is not a solo act.

Neither is ours.

As a kingdom people, we must be a kindred people, and it's the Spirit who unifies us. He empowers each of us to rise above our potential and take our place in God's mission with courage and confidence. We must not let the enemy isolate us in a fog of insecurity. Moses trusted the Lord with his vulnerabilities, and the Spirit provided a community to partner with him. He will do the same for us.

If God is challenging you to step up as a leader in your sphere of influence, then trust him. If He is calling you to persevere when all you want to do is quit, lean on him. Lace up your shoes, take that first step, and embrace the road before you.

Even if you're not sure you will succeed.

Even if you've tried before and failed.

There will be days the race runs you ragged. There may be days depression suffocates your soul, and you can't see any way forward. Follow Moses' example. Call upon the Spirit who hears the fears you can't even put into words (Rom 8:26). He will rescue you from the brinks of isolation and restore your battered heart. You are never truly alone; the Cultivator of community is with you, and his presence is power. That's who he is, and that's why he's worth trusting.

DIGGING DEEPER:

- Describe an area of your life where you've experienced the fear of failure.

- How might your life look differently without that fear?

- The author wrote, "The Spirit's story is not a solo act. Neither is ours. As a kingdom people, we must be a kindred people." What do you think about this statement?

- In what ways do kingdom people struggle to live this out, and why do you suppose that is?

- Identify one step you can you take to cultivate a more authentic kinship among your small group or church community.

- This chapter revealed the Spirit as the Cultivator of community. How does knowing this aspect of his personality encourage you to trust him more? And how might that trust transform your life?

Chapter Four

Othniel and the Champion of Second Chances

Judges 3:7–11

Conflict interrupts life like an uninvited house guest bursting through the door and tossing our agenda for the day out the window. It's unwanted, uncomfortable, and often unfair. You're probably experiencing some degree of conflict in at least one area of your life right now. It could be co-worker conflict, marital conflict, parenting conflict, church conflict, spiritual conflict, friendship conflict, or financial conflict just to name a few. Sometimes we reap strife sown by our own poor choices, and sometimes we find ourselves caught in the crossfires of other people's conflict. Neither scenario is easy to navigate.

Throughout the Old Testament, Israel experienced both. Enslaved without just cause by a fearful Pharaoh, the Jewish people struggled for survival and prayed for a savior. Efforts to reconcile the harsh reality of an unfair situation with faith in a good God generated substantial spiritual conflict. The burden of bondage bred tension between families and that relational pressure eventually erupted in all-out brawls. In every arena of their lives, spiritual, emotional, and physical, Israel understood what it felt like to be the collateral damage in someone else's conflict.

As noted in the previous chapter, God responded to their plight with a man named Moses. He led the people out of slavery into the Promised Land. Once freed from Pharaoh's heavy hand, however, Israel resisted God's authority and rebelled against his rules. They abandoned him for the worship of idols, ignoring his cautionary reminders of the consequences that would follow. Just as God warned, conflict erupted between Israel and the surrounding nations. The Jewish people eventually lost their freedom to Aram foreigners, and this time they had no-one to blame but themselves. They suffered under an oppression of their own making.

For eight years the sun rose upon a people subjugated as a result of their own sinful choices. For eight years the sun set to the sound of their repentant pleading. Forgive us, Yahweh. Rescue us, Yahweh. Restore us once again!

> "When they cried out to the Lord, he raised up for them a deliverer, Othniel son of Kenaz, Caleb's younger brother, who saved them" (Judg 3:9).

God was just in his reprimand and generous in his redemption. As he delivered Israel from Pharaoh's hand by way of a man named Moses, he would now deliver them from Aram oppression through a man named Othniel. Although Scripture offers minimal backstory on Othniel, we find the following tidbit tucked into the narrative of Joshua:

> "From Hebron, Caleb drove out the three Anakites— Sheshai, Ahiman and Talmai, the sons of Anak. From there he marched against the people living in Debir (formerly called Kiriath Sepher). And Caleb said, 'I will give my daughter Aksah in marriage to the man who attacks and captures Kiriath Sepher.' Othniel son of Kenaz, Caleb's brother, took it; so Caleb gave his daughter Aksah to him in marriage" (Josh 15:14–17).

We also discover in 1 Chronicles 4:13 that Othniel, of the tribe of Judah, fathered two sons, Hathath and Meonothai. Aside from his role as warrior and father, however, Othniel's entire story is summed up in the two verses that follow his appointment as God's chosen man to fight the enemy and restore Israel's freedom.

> "The Spirit of the Lord came on him, so that he became Israel's judge and went to war. The Lord gave Cushan-Rishathaim king of Aram into the hands of Othniel, who overpowered him. So, the land had peace for forty years, until Othniel son of Kenaz died" (Judg 3:10–11).

Despite the brevity of this description, Othniel's partnership emphasizes an essential aspect of the Spirit's nature. His interaction reveals a Spirit of second chances, a Spirit willing to forgive and restore. Israel experienced God's redemption before, but they still rejected him. They betrayed the one who brought them up out of Egypt and offered their hearts in worship to other gods instead. Only when their unfaithfulness led to eight years of enslavement did they fall to their knees and repent of their rebellion. Despite Israel's poor choices, the Spirit extended his powerful hand to help them escape the pit of sin's entanglements. He enabled them to experience the peaceful freedom of those whose chains had been broken.

It's worthwhile to note that the Spirit didn't ride in on a white horse and single-handedly defeat Israel's oppressors. He moved through the obedience of Othniel, through the willing heart of an ambitious warrior, to conquer the enemy together and set the captives free. Once again, we uncover an emphasis on community. Though he's powerful enough to stage a successful rescue on his own, the Spirit chose to partner with people instead. He empowers redemption by working in relationship with the repentant.

In a world flooded with spiritual, relational, and physical conflict, we're desperate for a Spirit of second chances, too. Even the best of us are still works in progress (Phil 1:6). We make mistakes. Sometimes really big, really awful, really impactful ones. Just like Israel, we rebel against the God who loves us. We worship busy schedules and set our relationship with him to the side. We worship the prestige associated with certain positions and compromise our faith to maintain that power. We worship ourselves and sacrifice Christlikeness for what's comfortable and pleasing in the moment.

Conflict is a part of our world. It can surface in our closest relationships, alienating us from others until we feel completely alone. It can seep into our churches, severing our sense of community and spoiling our witness with petty feuding that spills into fodder for public gossip.

Sometimes we're caught up in conflict through no fault of our own, but more often than not we encounter conflict because we've made bad decisions or sinful choices. Those are times we're especially susceptible to getting stuck in patterns of ongoing conflict. We can fall into the trap of a victim mentality and fail to hold ourselves accountable for our part in the predicament, however small it may be. Like Adam and Eve, we find someone else to blame. Though we plead for rescue, we're reluctant to admit our wrong or give up our sin. As we've discovered in earlier chapters, we cannot have both. Sin and the Spirit, like oil and water, do not mix.

Sin comes with a cost. It carries consequences and begets bondage. While the Spirit does not spare us the penalty of our own sinful choices, he does not abandon us amidst them either. He draws near and partners with us for deliverance. Israel suffered in captivity for years before finally falling to their knees and fighting for their life. Their deliverance required more than an apology; it took action. The Spirit empowered Othniel to lead the charge, but Israel had to choose to follow. They had to fight.

We face a similar decision.

We are creatures of comfort. We want the easy way out. We want the road of least resistance, but the path from conflict to peace, from turmoil to tranquility, often begins at the edge of a battlefield. Israel's second chance hinged on their choice to engage, and so does ours. We can partner with the Spirit and declare war on the sin that enslaves us, or we can remain in the clutches of conflict, foolishly awaiting an easier way out.

Israel wasted eight years, and that is tragic, but their willingness to partner with the Spirit ushered in a forty-year stretch of peace. We can learn from their success as much as we can from their mistakes. It's never too late to turn back to God. We need not resign ourselves to a lot in life fashioned by our own poor choices. We can repent. We can recognize the Spirit for who he, a Champion of second chances, and partner with him to bring about peace. He is able; we must be willing.

> "The mind governed by the flesh is death, but the mind governed by the Spirit is life and peace" (Rom 8:6).

Othniel's name meant "lion of God." I find it wonderfully ironic that the Spirit used a lion to usher in peace! Othniel, a son of Judah, a lion of Judah, fought with supernatural strength to secure forty years of freedom from enemy oppression. Scripture later references another Lion of Judah who also fought for the salvation of his people but whose victory achieved an even richer peace.

> "Then one of the elders said to me, 'Do not weep! See, the Lion of the tribe of Judah, the Root of David, has triumphed. He is able to open the scroll and its seven seals.' Then I saw a Lamb, looking as if it had been slain, standing at the center of the throne, encircled by the four living creatures and the elders. And they sang a new song, saying: 'You are worthy to take the scroll and to open its seals because you were slain, and with your blood you purchased for God persons from every tribe and language and people and nation'" (Rev 5:5–6, 9).

Othniel's story is a but a blip on the Old Testament timeline, but his partnership with the Spirit finds meaningful reflections in the greater narrative of a Lion who saved his people from their sins, a Lion slain like a Lamb, the crucified Christ. He broke down the barriers between humankind and a holy God ushering in an eternal, spiritual peace. He empowered relational reconciliation between Jew and Gentile to create a unified people of God with men and women from every tribe, tongue, and nation.

> "Now in Christ Jesus you who once were far away have been brought near by the blood of Christ. For he himself is our peace, who has made the two groups one and has destroyed the barrier, the dividing wall of hostility. For

through him we both have access to the Father by one Spirit" (Eph 2:13–14, 18).

"And you also were included in Christ when you heard the message of truth, the gospel of your salvation. When you believed, you were marked in him with a seal, the promised Holy Spirit, who is a deposit guaranteeing our inheritance until the redemption of those who are God's possession—to the praise of his glory" (Eph 1:13–14).

Victory is already ours, and that deliverance stretches beyond our lifetime on Earth into eternity like the ultimate second chance. The Spirit is our seal guaranteeing that anticipated completion. We can live confident in in our future perfection, but we have yet to experience the fullness of that reality. We remain works in progress. We still live in a conflicted world of lost and broken people.

The Spirit that empowered Othniel to wage war against Israel's oppressors remains the advocate of the repentant, the warrior of the willing. He does not cower in the face of conflict. He encourages his people to confront, to fight, to overcome. When our sinful nature rears its ugly head, we can cling to the Spirit of second chances and find deliverance. When we see others suffering in the self-inflicted wake of rebellion, we can partner with him as vessels of peace to draw them towards redemption, too.

DIGGING DEEPER:

- Identify one area you're currently experiencing some degree of conflict. What might the first step in partnering with the Spirit for peace in that situation look like?
- What could potentially hold you back from taking that step?
- What is the likely outcome if you do not take that step?
- What if you do?
- Do you think it's harder to accept a second chance when you've messed up or extend a second chance to someone else who's made a mistake? Why so?

- How does the Spirit help with both scenarios above (accepting and extending second chances)?

- This chapter revealed the Spirit as a Champion of second chances. How does knowing this aspect of his personality encourage you to trust him more? And how might that trust transform your life?

Chapter Five

Gideon and the Author of Impossible Scripts

Judges 6–7

L ife rarely moves forward in straightforward fashion. Instead, it unfolds as a series of forks in the road, and it's up to us to choose which path we'll follow. We decide between careers. We determine which relationships take priority. We decline one pursuit in favor of another, all without the benefit of guaranteed outcomes. We can compare costs and benefits, seek counsel, and pray for wisdom, but we rarely know exactly how the pathway forward will develop until future potential becomes present reality.

Not so for Israel. Following their rescue from Egypt, God identified two possible futures for the newly freed people. The direction they chose would determine which future they experienced. It would impact their children, livestock, land, and even political relations with neighboring nations. Simply put, their faithfulness guaranteed a blessed life, their unfaithfulness, a cursed one.

> "All these blessings will come on you and accompany you
> if you obey the Lord your God: You will be blessed in the
> city and blessed in the country. The fruit of your womb
> will be blessed, and the crops of your land and the young

of your livestock—the calves of your herds and the lambs of your flocks. The Lord will grant that the enemies who rise up against you will be defeated before you" (Duet 28:2–7).

Walk faithfully, and they would know peace, prosperity, and protection. That was God's promise. Should Israel reject his terms and follow the other path, however, they would face a very different fate.

"You will be cursed in the city and cursed in the country. The fruit of your womb will be cursed, and the crops of your land, and the calves of your herds and the lambs of your flocks. The Lord will cause you to be defeated before your enemies. You will be unsuccessful in everything you do; day after day you will be oppressed and robbed, with no one to rescue you" (Duet 28:16–18, 25–29).

God affirmed Israel's freedom to choose their pathway forward. They could walk in faithfulness, or they could forsake him and follow other gods. Their decision determined which version of the future they encountered. As we discovered in the previous chapter, Israel rebelled against their deliverer. They traded blessing for bondage and found themselves enslaved by a foreign regime just as God had warned. When they repented, however, the Spirit partnered in relationship with the warrior Othniel to secure their freedom and restore peace.

Unfortunately, lessons learned in the fiery heat of crisis often fade with the passing of time. Distanced from the disastrous consequences of their sin, Israel allowed complacency to creep back in among the community. They drifted from the pathway of faithful obedience and descended into full-blown rebellion once again. They suffered defeat at the hands of their enemies, and when they cried out in repentance, God graciously redeemed them. Eventually, however, the same cycle of complacency and sin repeated itself, and Israel found themselves in captivity again and again.

During the fourth round of Israelite rebellion, God allowed the Midianites, a nation of nomads and desert dwellers, to invade the land, spoil the crops, and slaughter the livestock. Banished from cities and unsafe in the countryside, the Jewish people escaped to the cliffs and caves where they carved out a life of rugged survival. One such Israelite, Gideon, spent several years living this way before an unexpected partnership with the Spirit wrote a whole new script for his future. Scripture introduces him in a scene that reveals just how difficult daily life for the Israelite exiles had become.

> "The angel of the Lord came and sat down under the oak in Ophrah that belonged to Joash the Abiezrite, where his son Gideon was threshing wheat in a winepress to keep it from the Midianites" (Judg 6:11).

Threshing wheat was a typical Israelite chore, but Gideon's method deviated from the usual process. Harvesters ordinarily moved grain from the fields to a threshing floor, an open area often atop a hill for better exposure to the breeze. They arranged sheaves in a circular formation so that oxen could trample out the kernels of grain. If a family didn't own a pair of oxen, they dragged a heavy sled or cart with sharp pieces of stone attached to the bottom instead. Once that backbreaking process finished, workers tossed grain into the air so that the wind would blow away the chaff. The heavier kernels would fall to the ground making it easier to collect and use.

During enemy occupation, however, exposure in the open area of a threshing floor increased the risk of theft or worse. Gideon was forced to complete the task in a pit hewn from rock instead, wrestling to work in a winepress designed for containing grapes without the usual help of other workers or the wind. I picture Gideon in this scene with shoulders hunched and beads of sweat on his brow, his whole body wearied by the exhausting efforts to match the strength of an ox in too small a space.

I imagine his thoughts a torturous mix of anger and anxiety. Perhaps memories of past harvests played through his mind. In those days he simply strapped the family oxen in place for the grueling task of trampling out the grain. He stood tall atop the hill, pausing in the process from time to time to appreciate the breeze for its refreshment as much as its role in easing the task of separating the grain from the chaff.

That was then.

This was now.

Robbed of his livestock, Gideon struggled in his limited strength. Deprived of his land, he cowered in a pit for fear of being found. Weary, worried, and all alone, he toiled away in the winepress until the voice from an unexpected visitor interrupted his work.

> "When the angel of the Lord appeared to Gideon, he said, 'The Lord is with you, mighty warrior.'
>
> 'Pardon me, my lord,' Gideon replied, 'but if the Lord is with us, why has all this happened to us? Where are all his wonders that our ancestors told us about when they said, 'Did not the Lord bring us up out of Egypt?' But now the Lord has abandoned us and given us into the hand of Midian'" (Judg 6:12–13).

Gideon's scene stands in stark contrast to the angel's salutation. Of all the settings he could have chosen, the angel of the Lord engages Gideon while he's struggling in a winepress. It's hardly the portrait of a mighty warrior. Overtaxed by work meant for oxen, his weary muscles betrayed his lack of strength. Forced into hiding, he felt forgotten by God. Rather than an expression of reassurance, the angel's greeting probably stung like salt in a deeply-resented wound.

The context doesn't reveal the tone of Gideon's words, but we can probably recall a time in our own lives when an unwelcome disruption during an irksome task triggered a snappy, sarcastic response. We can infer irritation and read his words as cynical statements laced with scorn, or we can interpret his answer as the sincere but conflicted confession of a man struggling to keep faith in the face of severe suffering. Whether his response rose from a place of bitterness, brokenness, or a bit of both, it reveals Gideon's resistance to the messenger and his message.

Despite his skepticism, however, something about the greeting stirs the memory of a story Gideon often heard as a youth. The angel's greeting echoed the words once spoken to Moses from a burning bush, hence Gideon's reference to the wonders of the exodus. In that ancient tale the hero responded to the angel of the Lord with his own set of doubts. Called to deliver the Israelites from Egyptian slavery, he questioned his worthiness for such a role, but God assured him that he would not be alone. He answered Moses's insecurities with the promise of his presence.

When the angel assured Gabriel, "The Lord is with you," he called this story to mind. Rather than inspiring Gideon, however, the reference to God's presence seemed to dishearten the already worn-out, not so mighty warrior. Recalling past wonders of the exodus amidst the present weariness of exile only reminded him how far Israel had fallen. If God was with him, why didn't he spare him this hardship? Gideon had no miracles to marvel at, no hope of rescue, and no energy to waste on a stranger's sentimental stroll down memory lane. His work in the winepress awaited.

Undaunted by Gideon's resistance, the angel of Lord continued, "Go in the strength you have and save Israel out of Midian's hand. Am I not sending you?" (Judg 6:14).

Yet again, the angel echoes words once spoken to Moses, but Gideon explains the impossibility of a scenario in which he would ever be chosen to save Israel. First, he doesn't come from the right clan. He's from the half-tribe of Manasseh, and a brief history lesson reveals why that spawned such deep-seeded insecurity within Gideon.

The twelve tribes of Israel symbolized the twelve sons of Jacob, except for the half-tribe of Manasseh and the half-tribe of Ephraim. They represented the two sons born to Joseph in Egypt after he was sold into slavery by his brothers. Manasseh was technically a grandson rather than a full-blooded son of Jacob, and in a strange twist of fate, he was denied his rightful blessing as first-born and given secondary position behind his younger brother. His story dripped with familial dysfunction on several levels, and the stigma plagued future generations.

Even if the angel insisted on choosing a deliverer from the lesser of all twelve Israelite tribes, Gideon considered himself last on the list of potential candidates within his clan. He was not a man of prominence or prestige. He wasn't a leader or warrior. He was the weakest man of the weakest clan, the guy tasked with the grunt work of grinding grain in a winepress. That was his story. That was his script, and he'd resigned himself to it.

The angel listened to Gideon's objections and repeated his opening greeting with one subtle but significant difference. When he first appeared, he assured Gideon that the Lord was with him. Now he announces, "I will be with you, and you will strike down all the Midianites, leaving none alive" (v 16). The shift from third person to first catches Gideon's attention. Suddenly aware that there might be more to the unexpected stranger who spoke in shadows of past than he initially thought, Gideon replies.

> "'If now I have found favor in your eyes, give me a sign that it is really you talking to me. Please do not go away until I come back and bring my offering and set it before you.'
>
> And the Lord said, 'I will wait until you return.' Gideon went inside, prepared a young goat, and from an ephah of flour he made bread without yeast" (Judg 6:17–19).

For a time of scarcity, Gideon's generous sacrifice implies the value he now attributed to this strange visitor. An ephah of flour was about half a bushel, and Gideon understood firsthand the effort it took to thresh that amount of grain! When he returned and placed the provisions on a rock, the angel reached out the tip of his staff to touch the meat. Fire flared upwards, engulfing the offering and confirming Gideon's hunch that this stranger was no ordinary messenger. He cried out in distress, "Alas, Sovereign Lord! I have seen the angel of the Lord face to face" (v 22).

Thus the God who once called Moses from a burning bush now calls Gideon from a flaming rock. The angel instructs him to demonstrate his obedience by tearing down his father's altar to Baal, replacing it, and offering a burnt sacrifice in worship of the one, true God instead. The request presented Gideon with the first of several forks in the road on his journey to fulfill his high calling.

We aren't privy to any internal dialogue as he debated the two options before him, but given his dubious nature, I imagine a doubt or two surfaced.

If Gideon ignored the angel's instruction, he risked missing out on the unexpected role of a lifetime, one reflective of Moses himself. If he trusted the angel and tore down his father's altar, however, he risked the small but still significant security of family. The pathway of obedience invited him to venture out of the winepress and step into a whole new storyline, but the other route beckoned him to stick with the status quo he'd grown accustomed to.

As he wrestled with the decision before him, I wonder if Gideon questioned whether the angel really existed or if the whole interaction was merely a delusion of an overworked, overheated man struggling to match the muscle of an ox in the confines of a winepress? The stakes were too high, the risks too significant to linger long in the limbo land of doubt. Eventually he had to choose a course of action and face whatever outcome awaited. Gideon delayed his decision until a protective blanket of darkness settled over his family's dwelling, but dawn's light revealed the destruction of his father's idolatrous altar, just as the angel commanded.

That first step of obedience opened up a powerful partnership with the Spirit. Gideon's decision to choose faith over fear sent him down a path he never anticipated. Entrusted with his next set of marching orders, he obeyed again, this time without waiting for the cover of night.

> "Then the Spirit of the Lord came on Gideon, and he blew a trumpet, summoning the Abiezrites to follow him. He sent messengers throughout Manasseh, calling them to arms, and also into Asher, Zebulun, and Naphtali, so that they too went up to meet them" (Judg 6:34–35).

Clothed in the Spirit's supernatural power, Gideon calls the Israelite community together with the battle cry of a trumpet blast. It's a return to their roots, a reminder of the former, faithful Israel whose trumpeting tradition reflected obedience to God's decree. "When you go to war in your land against the adversary who attacks you, then you shall sound an alarm with the trumpets, that you may be remembered before the Lord your God and be saved from your enemies" (Num 10:9). It's a throwback to the glory days when Joshua fought the battle of Jericho, seven priests blew seven trumpets, and the walls came tumbling down.

The Hebrew verb describing the Spirit's presence with Gideon is the same term used for dressing or wearing. This Hebrew word, *labash*, surfaces back in Genesis 3:21 when God clothed Adam and Eve with animal skins and again in Exodus 29:5 when the ephod and holy linens were put on Aaron to identify him as the priest. The Spirit dressed Gideon with himself; he covered him with the strength he lacked to empower him for the role he never imagined possible. The Spirit transformed the weakest man of the weakest clan into a brave warrior standing boldly in the open with battle horn in hand.

The trumpet blast signaled another victorious moment of faith over fear, and Israel responded in kind. For a nation banished to struggle for survival among cliffs and caves, the renewed experience of brotherhood bolstered conviction and confidence. Countrymen streamed into camp by the hundreds, gathering as one to oppose the Midianites. The final count of Israelite soldiers topped out at thirty-two thousand, and I imagine such a number astounded Gideon.

His story doesn't follow an easy path to victory from there, however. From dew-covered fleeces to doubt-ridden pleas for one more sign, he still struggled at times to accept the new narrative the Spirit was writing with his life. No sooner did he resolve one bout with insecurity than he faced another fork in the road, another test of trust.

> "The Lord said to Gideon, 'You have too many men. I cannot deliver Midian into their hands, or Israel would boast against me, 'My own strength has saved me.' Now announce to the army, 'Anyone who trembles with fear may turn back and leave Mount Gilead'" (Judg 7:2–3).

First God asked Gideon to risk what little security he found amongst family by tearing down his father's altar. Then he challenged him to lead the charge against the Midianites by rallying Israelite troops with a trumpet blast, a veritable death wish during enemy occupation! Now God wanted him to dismiss two-thirds of the military before they even reached the battlefield and reduce the fighting force to a mere ten thousand men. Gideon's new narrative grew more and more impossible with each successive step, but his choice to trust God anyways solidified a stronger partnership with the Spirit.

God continued whittling down the number of warriors until less than one percent of the original army remained. Gideon stared at the three-hundred soldiers left standing and determined to keep following God by faith. As darkness consumed daylight, subtle stirrings of the small, sober group echoed across the emptiness of the once-bustling campsite. Now more than ever one might expect Gideon to wrestle with doubts or seek another sign, but Scripture records no such request.

Gideon had grown, but God offered one final sign anyways. He instructed him to draw close enough to the Midianite camp to overhear the men. If Gideon obeyed, he would hear a message from the mouths of his enemies that would reassure him of Israel's forthcoming victory. The risky venture would place him in a precarious position, but a Spirit-clothed Gideon once again chose faith over fear. He descended into the valley and for the first time caught sight of the vast army he was up against.

> "The Midianites, the Amalekites, and all the other eastern people had settled in the valley, thick as locusts. Their camels could no more be counted than the sand on the seashore" (Judg 7:12).

Theoretically knowing the odds are stacked against you and visually encountering that overwhelming reality are two very different experiences. In comparison to the enemy soldiers blanketing the valley as far as the eye can see, Gideon's battalion of three hundred was but a drop in the bucket. Faced with the insurmountable likelihood of success, few would blame him for scurrying back to camp and signaling a full-fledged retreat, but Gideon pressed forward, right up to the fringes of the enemy encampment.

> "Gideon arrived just as a man was telling a friend his dream. 'I had a dream,' he was saying. 'A round loaf of barley bread came tumbling into the Midianite camp. It struck the tent with such force that the tent overturned and collapsed.'
>
> His friend responded, 'This can be nothing other than the sword of Gideon, son of Joash, the Israelite. God has given the Midianites and the whole camp into his hands'" (Judg 7:13–14).

The nameless friend of an enemy combatant connected the symbolism of the barley loaf with Israel, the original cultivators of the soil, and the overturned tent the with the Midianite invaders who destroyed their crops. The story of Gideon's partnership with the Spirit began in an unconventional setting for threshing wheat, and now it peaks with the ironic imagery of grain-baked bread symbolizing certain victory over the very ones he once cowered from in the winepress. A God sovereign enough to orchestrate such a perfectly timed moment was worthy of Gideon's unrestrained trust. The encouragement ignited an eagerness within, and after bowing in worship, Gideon bolted back to his handful of warriors bellowing, "Get up! The Lord has given the Midianite camp into your hands" (Judg 7:15).

Armed with trumpets and torches hidden in jars of clay, the Israelite battalion moved into position. At his signal three hundred horns thundered across the valley. Clay jars shattered, and the sudden flash of fiery torches set the sky ablaze. The Israelites shouted in unison, "A sword for the Lord and for Gideon!" (v 20).

Every unsteady step of his story led the unlikely hero to this moment of impossible triumph. Called from a stone pit to save his people, clothed by the Spirit of God himself, Gideon drank in the surreal scene. The bravado of three-hundred brothers fighting for their homeland filled his ears. The chaos of enemies scrambling to flee, turning on one another in bewilderment, played out before his eyes like ancient war stories of old.

Gideon never dared to dream his life could include such an incredible chapter until the day a stranger interrupted his work in the winepress. From coward to conqueror, he experienced the Spirit as the Author of impossible scripts. He learned to trust him wholeheartedly and the resulting partnership, forged by faith and fueled by conviction, set his world on fire in the best possible way.

The goal of Gideon's script rewrite was not personal glory or gain but the rescue and restoration of God's chosen people. The once-upon-a-time pit dweller prevailed against unbeatable odds by way of the Spirit to reunite Israel in the shared worship of the one true God. Like those before him, his story emphasizes the Spirit's heart for community. It inspires us to trust the Spirit when we face our own fork in the road opportunities, when he calls us to leave the confines of the winepress and embrace a new storyline with untold possibilities.

Like Gideon, our invitation usually requires an act of allegiance, a step of faith. Even after our initial decision to partner with the Spirit, the road may divide again and again just like it did for Gideon. Each time we must choose which path we will follow. We can trust the security of the status quo, or we can believe in the Author of impossible scripts.

Trusting the Spirit's direction for our story may collide with the narratives we've grown accustomed too. God's message countered Gideon's view of himself from the very beginning. Mighty warrior versus weary man in a winepress. Heroic savior versus son of the slighted half-tribe. His lot in life was one of bitterness and brokenness, his sense of self as beaten down as the grains beneath his feet, but he chose to look past his present storyline and embrace potential made possible only by partnering with the Spirit.

Letting go of those old narratives requires vulnerability, but the reward is victory, and that victory ripples outward to benefit those around us. We may face reoccurring doubts. We may struggle with past insecurities, and that's okay! Partnership with the Spirit is not a pathway to perfection but a relationship in which our imperfect souls move in sync with the Divine towards a destiny we never dreamed possible.

God didn't force Gideon to leave his pit; he won't compel our obedience either. We are free to follow whichever pathway we want, but our decision affects the future chapters of our life. The Spirit urges us to choose bravery and trust him as the Author of impossible scripts. He sees the whole story, from messy beginnings to victorious end, and he promises his presence with each and every step.

DIGGING DEEPER:

- In what ways can you relate to Gideon?
- How would you describe the "winepress" in your life?
- What obstacles might prevent you from stepping out of the winepress and into a new narrative?
- How do you see God growing Gideon with each new fork in the road?
- After Gideon accepted his new role, the story got worse! God shrunk his army again and again causing Gideon to wrestle with doubts. How can you learn from his example of faithfulness against all odds?
- This chapter revealed the Spirit as the Author of impossible scripts. How does knowing this aspect of his personality encourage you to trust him more? And how might that trust transform your life?

Chapter Six

Jephthah and the Redeemer of the Rejected

Judges 11:1–33

Twice a month our small group meets for brunch and bible study. We typically begin with a light-hearted icebreaker, and last month's question prompted members to share their favorite part of high school. The first person piped up with a grin and quipped, "Getting to leave after the final bell!"

We chuckled together in shared understanding, flashing back to our own bittersweet memories of lockers, funky lunches, and the drama of teenage social dynamics. Whether you got picked last for dodgeball or lived the dream as an all-star quarterback, helped backstage or scored the lead role in the school play, thrived as an honors student, struggled to pass, or landed somewhere in the middle, you had a place in the social hierarchy that ruled the hallowed halls of high school. You might not have cared enough about popularity to campaign for prom queen or king, but you wanted to fit in with your circle of friends. You wanted to belong. We all did.

And we still do.

Peer pressure doesn't disappear after graduation. From junior associates jockeying for their first promotion to senior level executives engrossed in power struggles for top dog position, navigating the social strata of the working world is exhausting. It's the high school drama of securing a spot at the cool kids' table all over again, the pressure-cooker pursuit of popularity that never really ends.

This drive to earn recognition for who we are and what we offer the world reveals our desire for significance. We want to be wanted. It's part of our God-ordained design and one of the more wonderful ways we reflect his nature. After all, he is three Persons in one. His relational heart beats in perfect rhythm with community, and once upon a time ours did, too.

As we've discussed before, God wired humankind with the social blueprint to connect with others from the very beginning. Adam and Eve were two perfect peas in a pod, walking and talking in pure harmony with God. When sin entered the scene, however, it disrupted that rhythm, and we've been relationally out of sync ever since. Our post-paradise struggle to reconnect and restore lost intimacy leaves us vulnerable to the threat of rejection. From break-ups to boardroom dismissals, first date flops to failed promotions, rejection wreaks havoc on our soul. It threatens our sense of self, suggesting that we aren't as valuable or worthwhile as we want to be.

Rejection is part of life after the fall. It's part of being human, and no matter how old we get, it still hurts. We may wonder how different life would be if we hadn't been turned down for certain opportunities. We lament regrets we wish we could un-write, rejections that benched us from the game we felt born to play.

Some of us can pinpoint entire chapters of our life written in response to rejection. Jephthah certainly could. In fact, it scripted the bulk of his story. Resented by the ones who should have loved him, he lived like an outsider from the day he was born. By all appearances his destiny seemed set, his lot in life pre-determined, but later chapters reveal the redemptive potential of rejection-laced problems. Abandonment is a powerful pen, but the Spirit is stronger. The script he wrote with Jephthah's life lives on as a testament to forgiveness-driven transformation. As we study his interaction with the Holy Spirit, we discover the Spirit's power to reroute a destiny steeped in scandal towards a place of reconciliation and purpose.

Jephthah's tale unfolds amidst yet another cycle of Israelite rebellion. After eighteen years of persecution at the hands of the Philistines and Ammonites, the Israelites repented and begged God to rescue them. In the past, God responded with partnerships between the Spirit and seasoned warriors like Othniel as well as the unlikely heroes like Gideon. This time he didn't choose the strongest or the weakest; instead, he cultivated a partnership that reflected the complicated dynamics of his relationship with Israel.

God chose a man who knew what rejection felt like, a man whose family unfairly abandoned him just like Israel rejected Yahweh. He chose Jephthah, the firstborn of an affluent father whose social status was sabotaged by the illegitimacy of his birth. The scandal of his conception colored his childhood, and while his siblings enjoyed the esteem afforded their family as members of the wealthy elite, he lived as an unwanted outcast.

> "Jephthah the Gileadite was a mighty warrior. His father was Gilead; his mother was a prostitute. Gilead's wife also bore him sons, and when they were grown up, they drove Jephthah away. 'You are not going to get any inheritance in our family,' they said, 'because you are the son of another woman.' So Jephthah fled from his brothers and settled in the land of Tob, where a gang of scoundrels gathered around him and followed him" (Judg 11:1–3).

Jephthah didn't have to wonder about his role in the family; they made his place very clear. You do *not* belong. You are *not* wanted. Leave, and never come back.

That depth of rejection can develop quite the drive within a person to prove himself. Scorned by his own flesh and blood, Jephthah found a new band of brothers, a flock of fellow misfits willing to follow his lead. Over time he established himself as a competent and courageous commander. Word of his reputation

45

spread far and wide, eventually reaching his hometown, but his family refused to reconsider their decision. Despite his recognition among neighboring communities as a fierce fighter and formidable leader, his siblings still saw him as the disgraceful spawn of a dirty prostitute.

Until tragedy struck.

Israel fell under siege. The very ones who scorned Jephthah sought him out for help. They needed his strength and strategy to save their land from Ammonite attack.

> "'Come,' they said, 'be our commander, so we can fight the Ammonites.'
>
> Jephthah said to them, 'Didn't you hate me and drive me from my father's house? Why do you come to me now, when you're in trouble?'
>
> The elders of Gilead said to him, 'Nevertheless, we are turning to you now; come with us to fight the Ammonites, and you will be head over all of us who live in Gilead'" (Judg 11:6–8).

I can only imagine the cyclone of thoughts churning in Jephthah's mind at this unexpected encounter. His last memory of these men dripped with shame and disgrace. They chased him away from house and home, and now they had the audacity to reappear without apology and ask for his help. No doubt the temptation for revenge rose to mind. As the commander of a renowned army, he certainly had the upper hand!

This perfect opportunity for payback coincided with another invitation, however, a chance to take the high road, to forgive his childhood tormentors and write a worthier ending to his narrative. The outsider could return. The unwanted warrior could save the day. The rejected son of harlot could embrace his new role as hometown hero.

Talk about a defining moment! His response to the unforeseen plot twist would forever move his story forward in one of two different directions. Either he abandoned those who abandoned him first, severing family ties once and for all, or he accepted their offer to lead the clan into battle and hoped they fulfilled their end of the bargain.

Jephthah feared the elders might deny him the promised position as head of Gilead even if he defeated the enemy. For a man who learned early on in life that people will lie, cheat, fail and forsake you, agreeing to help required a significant overhaul of the bunker-style barriers wrapped around his heart. It opened him up to more potential rejection. Anyone who's endured betrayal understands the battle of forgiveness; it's scary to loosen the self-protective layers and dare to trust again.

> "Jephthah answered, 'Suppose you take me back to fight the Ammonites and the Lord gives them to me—will I really be your head?'
>
> The elders of Gilead replied, 'The Lord is our witness; we will certainly do as you say.' So Jephthah went with the elders of Gilead, and the people made him head and commander over them. And he repeated all his words before the Lord in Mizpah" (Judg 11:9–11).

While Scripture doesn't explicitly describe the relationship between Jephthah and Yahweh, his response indicates some measure of faith. The elders' request roused his suspicions, but their appeal to the Lord as their witness resonated with something within him. Despite understandable reservations, Jephthah agreed and confirmed his intentions by returning to Mizpah where he "repeated all his words before the Lord."

This phrase astounds me. I get chills every time I read it! The one who fled his childhood home, a hellish reality of relentless rejection, now stands in the very place of his wounding, and he worships. Jephthah worships. He states his truth before Almighty God, declaring his intentions to battle on behalf of the very ones who abused and abandoned him. What a stunning portrait of forgiveness in action. The elders and his ruthless brothers may not have warranted such loyalty, but Jephthah believed God did, and he was willing to lay down his own life if necessary.

"The Spirit of the Lord came on Jephthah. He crossed Gilead and Manasseh, passed through Mizpah of Gilead, and from there he advanced against the Ammonites" (Judg 11:29).

Of all the potential rescuers living in Israel at that time, the Spirit chose to rewrite the storyline of an unwanted son betrayed by family and banished to the fringes of society. The Spirit we met at the dawn of creation, the one who saw potential in unlikely places, recognized in Jephthah what his family failed to realize. He saw the heart and soul of a fighter, brave enough to face one enemy while forgiving another.

Jephthah's yes forever altered the course of his life and the lives of those he protected. By partnering with the Spirit, he secured freedom for the whole Israelite community, but his road to redemption was not without risk. The same is true for us today. Partnering with the Spirit to script a scene change for our story requires trust. We must believe that his pen is mightier than the voices of our past. We must trust his ability to redeem what others have rejected, and that means granting him access to every piece of our heart, especially the ones we've buried beneath layers of self-protective bubble wrap.

It's hard to trust when we've been hurt. And we've all been hurt. We've all encountered rejection.

The Spirit understands; he's felt that way, too. Israel abandoned God time and time again. He rescued them through men like Moses and judges like Othniel, Gideon, and Jephthah. As we will discover in chapters ahead, God later raised up kings and prophets. Eventually he even sent his very own son, and they crucified him.

The cross was the epitome of rejection, but redemption had the final word in Christ's story. He is "the stone the builders rejected, which has become the cornerstone" (Acts 4:11; Ps 118:22). Redemption can rewrite the emphasis of your story, too. That's the transformative power of forgiveness. And it can begin right now.

The elders never offered Jephthah an apology for the past, at least not one that Scripture records. There is no touching scene of reconciliation between him and his brothers. Without being asked by the guilty parties, he still chose to forgive, not in words but through action. When efforts at diplomacy with enemy leaders failed, he rode into battle on behalf of those who wronged him and found redemption in the process. He witnessed a Spirit-fueled triumph, and his faith earned him a place in Hebrews hall of fame (Heb 11:32).

Some wounds linger unresolved; some strands still dangle loose despite our efforts to wrap up certain chapters of our life and finally move on. The Spirit gathers these rejected pieces of our past and weaves them together into something purposeful by partnering with us to move forward in faith. He knows the heartache of rejection. He is worthy of our complete trust, but we must let him in and let him lead. Lowering the barricades around our heart can feel scary, but that is how the healing begins.

We've seen the Spirit partner with the strongest, the weakest, and now the unwanted. Whichever category you may find yourself in, understand that he wants to partner with you. He knows your past, he knows your fears, and he chooses you anyways. If you're willing, you, like Jephthah, can experience the joy of redemption when places of wounding become places of worship. It happens in partnership with the Spirit, the Redeemer of the rejected.

DIGGING DEEPER:

- The author wrote, "We must believe his pen is mightier than the voices of our past." In what ways does this statement resonate with you?

- Why is action-oriented forgiveness so difficult to live out?

- How does unforgiveness in one relationship affect our freedom in other relationships?

- "With the Spirit places of wounding become places of worship." What might this look like in your life?

- This chapter revealed the Spirit as the Redeemer of the rejected. How does knowing this aspect of his personality encourage you to trust him more? And how might that trust transform your life?

Chapter Seven

Samson and the Just Deliverer

Judges 13–16

As an adoptive parent, I celebrate the unexpected ways God weaves a family together. We frequently talk with our son about God's sovereign plan, framing his adoption as part of the storyline purposefully pieced together to work all things together for his good. I treasure the moment my arms first welcomed him home, and the photo of me at the hospital in blue scrubs holding him next to his birth mother so we could marvel at his teeny, tiny face together is an absolute favorite! While I cannot imagine a world in which I am not this boy's mother, I recognize the bittersweet nature of adoption. For better or worse, my son's first chapters were written without any input or say-so from him.

I suppose the same is true for all of us. No-one really controls the circumstances they are born into. We don't decide on the biological, psychological, or situational influences that shape our childhood experiences and impact future chapters of our life. Jephthah, who we met in the previous chapter, and Samson, whose story we're about to explore, both understood this dynamic. Set in motion from the time of conception, their stories follow two very different courses towards two very different destinies. One birth stemmed from scandalous beginnings, the other fulfilled angelic foretelling; Jephthah was a son of promiscuity and Samson a son of promise.

While Jephthah's difficulties originated externally from the rejection of his family, Samson's problems stemmed from an internal struggle with his selfish desires. Born into a sacred calling, he repeatedly fell into sin. Before we skip too far ahead in his story, however, let's review the events that impacted Samson's life before he ever drew his first breath.

> "Again the Israelites did evil in the eyes of the Lord, so the Lord delivered them into the hands of the Philistines for forty years. A certain man of Zorah, named Manoah, from the clan of the Danites, had a wife who was childless, unable to give birth. The angel of the Lord appeared to her and said, 'You are barren and childless, but you are going to become pregnant and give birth to a son. Now see to it that you drink no wine or other fermented drink and that you do not eat anything unclean. You will become pregnant and have a son whose head is never to be touched by a razor because the boy is to be a Nazirite, dedicated to God from the womb. He will take the lead in delivering Israel from the hands of the Philistines'" (Judg 13:1–5).

For Israelite women, a barren womb implied divine disfavor. While I know the heart-sick sorrow of empty arms, I can only imagine the shame women endured in that culture. The overwhelming ocean of emotion accompanying infertility wreaks enough havoc on the heart without the additional weight of societal disgrace. Thus, the angel's announcement to Manoah's wife inspired happiness both for the fulfillment of maternal longings and freedom from the stigma of childlessness.

The prophecy regarding his future role further multiplied the expectant mother's joy. Not only would this son of promise deliver her from the burden of barrenness, but he would liberate Israel from the burden of Philistine oppression. Samson was born to lead, and his parents made a vow of dedication on his behalf before his birth.

The pledge bestowed upon Samson aligned him with the ancient order of Nazarites. This group adopted their name from the Hebrew term *nazir* which means consecrated one.[1] The vows of a Nazarite required strict adherence to three rules: abstain from wine or fruit of the vine including grapes and raisins, avoid proximity to corpses since they were considered unclean, and allow the hair to grow uncut for the duration of one's vow. These external indicators reflected the sincerity of one's commitment to the sacred vow, but at the completion of their pledge they would be released from these rules. In obedience to the angel, however, Samson's parents obliged him to a lifelong Nazarite vow.

> "The woman gave birth to a boy and named him Samson. He grew, and the Lord blessed him, and the Spirit of the Lord began to stir him" (Judg 13:24–25).

Scripture offers little insight into Samson's formative years aside from this early stirring of the Spirit. The Hebrew term translated as stirring, *pa'am*, means to thrust or compel. It surfaces elsewhere regarding dreams of pharaohs and kings which godly men interpreted. For example, in Genesis 41:8 Pharaoh awoke troubled by a dream which Joseph later interpreted as seven years of feast followed by seven years of famine. In Daniel 2:1–3, King Nebuchadnezzar experienced a similar troubling and sought out Daniel to interpret the dream. The Psalmist uses this term to describe his restless inability to sleep in 77:2–4. "When I was in distress, I sought the Lord; at night I stretched out untiring hands, and I would not be comforted. I remembered you, God, and I groaned; I meditated, and my spirit grew faint. You kept my eyes from closing; I was too troubled *(pa'am)* to speak."

Have you ever woken up from a dream so intense and lifelike that the anxious emotions lingered long after your eyes had opened? Sometimes those images haunt you no matter how many times you remind yourself it was just a nightmare. Perhaps Samson experienced something similar. Maybe the Spirit stirred Samson's protectiveness of the people he was purposed to lead by allowing

---

1. Harrison, *International Standard Bible Encyclopedia*, 501.

him to feel the suffering of his countrymen through troubling dreams.

Imagine waking in the dead of night, gasping for breath beneath the crushing weight of a father's grief over a daughter taken and abused by her Philistine captors. Imagine the haunting echo of a mother wailing over a wayward son lost to the intoxication of the Philistine's rampant drunkenness and debauchery. Imagine the seething anger of man toiling to repair a home or field trashed by Philistine cruelty. Vicariously experiencing the vivid emotions of his persecuted people through such visions would undoubtedly stir a passion for vengeance within Samson!

In whatever manner this "stirring" manifested itself in Samson's life, it helped prepare him for his future role as Israel's deliverer. The Spirit's influence competed with a rivaling force within this son of promise, however. Despite angelic prophecies and Nazarite vows, Samson struggled with sin. His lust for women led to rash decisions, and he failed to learn from the fallout of his mistakes.

His first encounter with seductive manipulation surfaces in Judges 14:1–20. While visiting the town of Timnah, he saw a Philistine woman and determined he must have her. Upon convincing his reluctant parents that she was indeed the one for him, he pledged to marry her and returned to the city for a feast of celebration. Along the way, Samson encountered a lion, and the Spirit of the Lord came so powerfully upon him that he tore it apart with his bare hands.

When he safely arrived in the city, Samson wagered a bet with a riddle inspired by the lion. If his bride's family answered correctly, he would gift them thirty sets of clothing, but if by week's end the puzzle still stumped them, Samson would win the clothes for himself. Three days passed without any progress in solving Samson's riddle, so the Philistines pressured his future wife to coax the answer from him.

> "Samson's wife threw herself on him, sobbing, 'You hate me! You don't really love me. You've given my people a riddle, but you haven't told me the answer.'

'I haven't even explained it to my father or mother,' he replied, 'so why should I explain it to you?' She cried the whole seven days of the feast. So on the seventh day, he finally told her, because she continued to press him. She, in turn, explained the riddle to her people" (Judg 14:16–17).

Bested by the Philistines through betrayal, Samson's blood boiled. As with the lion, the Spirit strengthened him, and he struck down thirty Philistine men, giving the clothes of the dead men in payment of the wager as promised. Still fuming, he returned to his father's house, and in his absence the Philistines gave his intended bride to another man. When Samson learned of the marriage, the news incited a second rampage.

"He went out and caught three hundred foxes and tied them tail to tail in pairs. He then fastened a torch to every pair of tails, lit the torches and let the foxes loose in the standing grain of the Philistines. He burned up the shocks and standing grain, together with the vineyards and olive groves" (Judg 15:4–5).

In an age of courtroom proceedings where lawyers engage in back-and-forth presentations of evidence and juries debate for endless hours before settling on verdicts, this portrait of instantaneous justice seems brutal, bloody, and uncivilized. It's unsettling to associate the Spirit with this type of violence, yet Scripture states he supplied Samson's strength. He empowered the vengeance against the Philistines.

The men Samson punished were not innocent victims, however. The Philistines engaged in exceptionally evil practices, even burning children in fires as sacrifices to honor their deities. They lived wicked lives, and God held them accountable for their offensive actions. The Spirit acted justly in empowering Samson to deliver the penalty of death they deserved. We know this is true because the Spirit is God, and God is always just.

"For all his ways are just; a God of faithfulness and without injustice, righteous and upright is he" (Deut 32:4).

"But the Lord abides forever; he has established his throne for judgment, and he will judge the world in righteousness" (Ps 9:7–8).

"For the Lord is a God of justice" (Isa 30:18).

The Spirit sovereignly worked through Samson to accomplish His just purposes, but eventually, Samson fell prey to his sinful pursuits. Failing to learn from his first go-around with seduction, he visited a prostitute in Gaza. The Philistines planned to capture him in the morning, but Samson's strength enabled him to escape unscathed (Judg 16:1–3).

He later fell in love with another woman, Delilah, who took a bribe from the Philistines to betray him into their hands. She repeatedly begged Samson to reveal the secret of his strength, but he only supplied her with false answers. Consequently the Philistines' attempts to capture him would inevitably fail. After three rounds a determined Delilah intensified her strategy.

> "Then she said to him, 'How can you say, 'I love you,' when you won't confide in me? This is the third time you have made a fool of me and haven't told me the secret of your great strength.' With such nagging, she prodded him day after day until he was sick to death of it. So he told her everything.
>
> 'No razor has ever been used on my head,' he said, 'because I have been a Nazirite dedicated to God from my mother's womb. If my head were shaved, my strength would leave me, and I would become as weak as any other man'" (Judg 16:15–17).

In partnership with the Spirit, Samson never once experienced physical weakness. He could tear apart lions and slaughter a small army with nothing but a donkey's jawbone. No brute or beast could bind him! Instead of honoring the source of his strength, however, Samson developed a sense of invincibility. He ignored his susceptibility to sin, and this failure to address his lustful desires and establish healthier, holier habits eventually led to his downfall.

The Spirit's presence in Samson's life was not a blank check for immorality. As already discussed, sin and the Spirit, like oil and water, do not mix. Samson repeatedly surrendered to temptation, and eventually the Lord gave him over to the path of his choosing. Delilah lured him to sleep in her lap, violated his Nazarite vow by cutting his hair, and delivered him into the hands of his enemies.

> "He awoke from his sleep and thought, 'I'll go out as before and shake myself free.' But he did not know that the Lord had left him. Then the Philistines seized him, gouged out his eyes and took him down to Gaza. Binding him with bronze shackles, they set him to grinding grain in the prison" (Judg 16:20–21).

Samson didn't even recognize the Lord's absence until it was too late. His spiritual blindness led to literal blindness. Born to deliver his people, he faced the humiliating reality of his own captivity instead.

Samson's fall from son of promise to prison slave speaks to sin's danger, but his story does not end in complete defeat. During a celebratory feast, the Philistines summoned their trophy of triumph to center stage for their entertainment. Under the guise of weakness, Samson requested that they place him between two pillars so he could lean on them.

> "Then Samson prayed to the Lord, 'Sovereign Lord, remember me. Please, God, strengthen me just once more'" (Judg 16:28).

With arms outstretched and a hand firmly placed upon each pillar, Samson pushed with all his might. The temple roof caved in, and death rained down on Israel's enemies. Though he perished among them, Samson died with renewed faith (Heb 11:32). He sacrificed his life in one final feat of justice.

Rather than a tale of linear spiritual success, Samson's narrative follows a split storyline revealing two essential aspects of the Holy Spirit's nature. First, it reminds us that perfection is not a prerequisite for partnership with the Spirit. He empowered justice for the wicked Philistines and freedom for captive Israel through a man plagued by temptation and prone to entrapment. The Spirit showcased his sovereignty by repurposing Samson's failures to accomplish a higher purpose.

Secondly, it reminds us that the Spirit is holy. Our toleration of sin, no matter how small, hampers the potency of his strength in our lives. Picture his power channeling through us like water flows through a pipe. When the pipe is free of debris, the water flows strong and steady; when layers of filth clog the pipeline, however, it restricts the flow to a mere trickle. Sin is the muck that clogs the pipe. It built up in Samson's life little by little until he completely cut himself off from the source of his strength. He didn't realize sin had severed his connection until it was too late.

Our world still stands in need of deliverance; spiritual bondage is causing catastrophic harm in our homes, our churches, and our communities. We can partner with the Spirit to liberate those held hostage by demons of their own making, but that requires us to recognize our susceptibilities, to understand that we are not invincible. Like Samson, we are prone to temptation. We cannot turn a blind eye to sin's presence in our lives; we must be vigilant watchmen over our own hearts.

> "Each person is tempted when they are dragged away by their own evil desire and enticed. Then, after desire has conceived, it gives birth to sin; and sin, when it is full-grown, gives birth to death" (Jas 1:14–15).

It's time to stop flirting along the fringes of Satan's territory, foolishly expecting we can play at the edge without danger of falling in. Too many well-intentioned couples walk down the aisle weighed down by the baggage of boundaries they never meant cross before their wedding day. Too many ministry leaders stumble away from scandal after swearing they'd never end up as one of the statistics they scoffed at in seminary. Too many born-again believers promise it'll just be one last drink, one last bet, one more little white lie, only it never really is.

We are not invincible.

We are not immune to sin.

We may not get caught right away, but eventually, the consequences catch up with us. Samson rejected the Spirit for sensual pleasures and paid the ultimate price. Though he's granted a final scene of faith, his story could have been so much more.

> "No temptation has overtaken you except what is common to mankind. And God is faithful; he will not let you be tempted beyond what you can bear. But when you are tempted, he will also provide a way out so that you can endure it" (1 Cor 10:13).

We will face temptation, but there is always a way out. We must stay connected to the Spirit. The Apostle Paul implored believers, "Do not quench the Spirit" (1 Thess 5:19). The term "quench" in this verse is the Greek verb *sbennymi* which means to stifle or extinguish.

Jesus used this word in Matthew 25:8 during his parable of the ten virgins awaiting the coming of the bridegroom. Five wisely brought extra oil in jars while the other five risked their lamps burning out (*sbennymi).* As the night went on, the five women who failed to bring extra oil had to leave and find more. Because of their careless attitude, they missed the celebration of the bridegroom's arrival and admittance into the wedding banquet.

When we give into temptation, we quench the Spirit. We allow sin to stifle his light in our lives. Just like the five foolish virgins in Jesus' parable, we're left in the dark.

Samson lived in this darkness long before his physical blindness. Sin extinguished the Spirit's strength in his life, and his story inspires us to choose differently. If we resist temptation and embrace a partnership with the Spirit, his presence will ripple outward in waves of deliverance. He liberates us from sin's shame and empowers us as vessels of rescue for others still trapped in spiritual bondage. Samson failed to learn from his mistakes in time, but it's not too late for us. We can choose the path of the Spirit. He is the just Deliverer, and he calls us to follow his lead in a world desperate for his freedom.

DIGGING DEEPER:

- "It's time to stop flirting along the fringes of Satan's territory, foolishly expecting we can play at the edge without danger of falling in." Where do you see the church "flirting along the fringes" today?

- What might this "flirting" look like in your own life?

- How can we protect against the illusion of invincibility that blinds us to our own susceptibility to sin?

- What hope does Samson's final scene offer?

- This chapter revealed the Spirit as the just Deliverer. How does knowing this aspect of his personality encourage you to trust him more? And how might that trust transform your life?

Chapter Eight

_____

Saul and the Source of Peace
1 Samuel 9–15

I quit my first high school job with every intention of honoring the obligatory two-week notice. After serving tacos all summer at a popular fast food chain, I scored a role in our school's fall musical and resigned from the restaurant to accommodate the rehearsal schedule. It took some effort, but I successfully juggled both responsibilities until my last shift coincided with practice and all efforts to trade hours with a co-worker fell short.

For a people-pleaser like me, that sixteen-year-old scenario triggered a sizeable guilt storm. Forced to choose between disappointing my taco boss or new play director, I felt trapped in a lose-lose situation. Eventually, I had to choose my priority, and I picked play practice, but the guilt of bailing on my final shift burdened me for longer than I care to admit.

I'd like to say I've matured beyond those people-pleasing tendencies, but my track record in leadership suggests otherwise. Sometimes I still spend more time than necessary toiling over minor decisions for fear of letting someone down. For example, as music director, the simple act of selecting one of the songs suggested by the congregation for a special occasion ties my stomach in knots. Saying yes to one means saying no to all the others. Heaven forbid my failure to pick someone's song sours their opinion of me! As irrational as such thinking may be, it's the way my brain automatically processes. While my fear-prone personality would happily avoid ever being in charge of anything, I invest intentional efforts in learning how to lead despite this natural inclination because I trust God's calling on my life.

Saul understood the internal complexities associated with reluctant leaders like me. His story lives on as a cautionary tale for people-pleasers who grapple with the gnawing reality that it's impossible to please everyone about everything all the time, especially in positions of leadership. Setting our course to the erratic sway of popular opinion renders us ineffective and forces us to prioritize the approval of others above God. If we can learn to trust his voice above the chorus competing for our attention, however, we can lead with a sound mind in harmony with the Holy Spirit.

Saul's refusal to learn crippled his leadership, and an autopsy of his errors offers valuable insights for leaders today. It reminds us to pursue God's glory, not our own, and more importantly for the purposes of this study, it reveals a valuable aspect of the Spirit's personality. Saul's story unveils the Spirit as the source of peace that frees us from the burden of fighting for people's approval.

Scripture first introduces Saul as a young man searching for his father's lost donkeys. After scouring the foothills of Ephraim, the district of Shalisha, and the territory of Benjamin to no avail, Saul suggested that the search party turn back lest his father's concern shift from missing donkeys to his missing son. The servants aiding in the quest offered an alternative solution, however. They knew a man of God named Samuel, a highly respected prophet who lived nearby. Perhaps he could inquire of God and determine the donkey's location so they could avoid returning home empty-handed. Saul agreed to the new plan without realizing that the temporary detour would reroute his entire future.

> "Now the day before Saul came, the Lord had revealed this to Samuel: 'About this time tomorrow I will send you a man from the land of Benjamin. Anoint him ruler over my people Israel; he will deliver them from the hand of

the Philistines. I have looked on my people, for their cry has reached me'" (1 Sam 9:15–16).

Saul's search for lost livestock led him down a path he did not plan for. The Spirit's ambitions for this young man far exceeded a mission for missing donkeys. Dazed and confused at the revelation of his royal appointment, he responded much like Gideon. He questioned God's choice saying, "Am I not a Benjamite, from the smallest tribe of Israel, and is not my clan the least of all the clans of the tribe of Benjamin?" (1 Sam 9:21).

Though Scripture describes Saul as standing a head taller than the other men, his confidence was in short supply. As his country's first king, he would pioneer the responsibilities of royalty and single-handedly forge the foundations of an Israelite monarchy. No previous ruler could mentor by example, no prior establishment offered the basic benefits of infrastructure or political routine, and Saul recoiled at the notion of building a kingdom from scratch.

Despite the young man's reluctance, Samuel anointed him with olive oil. He predicted that Saul would encounter three signs on his next journey, three confirmations of God's call on his life. First, he would hear from two men near the border of Benjamin that the missing donkeys had returned home and his father now worried over his absent son. Secondly, at the great tree of Tabor, he would meet a trio of men traveling to worship with goats and provisions. They would offer Saul two loaves of bread before continuing on their way. The final sign would occur in Gibeah with a parade of prophets playing all sorts of musical instruments.

The three signs came to pass precisely as promised, and Saul's storyline shifted in a significant way. He crossed paths with two men bearing a message of the donkeys' safe return. He met a trio who offered him two of their three bread loaves. He encountered a procession of prophets and experienced the presence of the Spirit in a manner reflective of another shift in leadership style when God appointed seventy elders to serve alongside Moses.

> "The Spirit of God came powerfully upon him, and he joined in their prophesying. When all those who had formerly known him saw him prophesying with the

prophets, they asked each other, 'What is this that has happened to the son of Kish? Is Saul also among the prophets?'" (1 Sam 10:10–11).

We learned earlier that uncharacteristic occurrences of prophetic speaking are one way through which the Spirit identifies his presence at crucial moments in Israelite history and humankind's overall storyline. Saul's royal appointment as the first king of Israel marked a noticeable change in the way God partnered with human leaders to guide his people. The prophetic activity in this verse signified the unique presence of the Spirit and assured the witnesses that he was indeed God's chosen man. As a mark of divine anointing, the experience should have reassured Saul, but Scripture records his hesitancy to embrace his new role in God's plan.

> "Now Saul's uncle asked him and his servant, 'Where have you been?'
>
> 'Looking for the donkeys,' he said. 'But when we saw they were not to be found, we went to Samuel.'
>
> Saul's uncle said, 'Tell me what Samuel said to you.'
>
> Saul replied, 'He assured us that the donkeys had been found.' But he did not tell his uncle what Samuel had said about the kingship" (1 Sam 10:14–16).

Saul suffered from a classic case of people-pleasing syndrome. Unsure of his family's response, he kept Samuel's message a secret. Perhaps he feared offending them. "So, you think you're better than us, that you deserve to be our king?" Or sounding like a crazy man. "I think you spent a little too much time out in the sun on that donkey search!" Maybe what he dreaded most was not their disbelief but their approval of Samuel's prophecy. If they trusted Samuel's message from God, they would expect Saul to rise to the role, and expectation opened the door for disappointment. Better to never be king at all than to try and let everyone down.

When Samuel later summoned Israel to Mizpah to reveal God's choice for king, Saul's secret came out. The reluctant leader hid among the supplies, but when the people found him, they dragged him up front. The crowd celebrated, cheering together, "Long live the king!" Sensing Saul's internal insecurities, however, several of the constituents questioned his ability to keep Israel safe (1 Sam 10:27). Their failure to offer gifts dishonored the new king, and though he neglected to confront them, their insolence lingered in the back of his mind.

Saul's struggle with people-pleasing only intensified when he assumed the throne. Public opinion wreaked havoc on his soul. If we fast-forward from coronation day, we discover an increasingly suspicious Saul. Hypersensitive to the slightest hint of disloyalty, he repeatedly compromised himself to secure the people's approval.

During one particularly tense chapter of his reign, the Philistines rallied against Israel with three thousand chariots, six thousand charioteers, and soldiers as "numerous as the sand on the seashore" (1 Sam 13:5). Fearful of such an intimidating force, the Israelite troops anxiously awaited Samuel's arrival to seek God's favor in battle. Saul knew that usurping the prophet's duty defied God's decree, but when his men began scattering, he panicked and ordered the offering himself. Unwilling to risk further questioning of his capabilities as commander-in-chief, he caved to peer pressure and disobeyed God.

No sooner did the smoke trail upwards then Samuel appeared and rebuked Saul's actions. Justifying his sin, Saul argued that his men were on the verge of mutiny. He blamed Samuel for failing to arrive at the scheduled time. He pointed out the spiritual nobility of seeking God's favor, but all his excuses fell on deaf ears. Samuel saw past the pretense. He understood that Saul's actions stemmed from fear, not faith. The new king's paranoia reflected his inability to trust the Spirit's power.

Despite Samuel's warnings that such defiance would cost him the kingdom, Saul continued prioritizing the opinions of others above obedience; he valued people's approval more than God's. His defiance against God's directives during an attack against the Amalekites several months later elicited more criticism from the prophet, but Saul again argued his defense. He rationalized his actions instead of confessing and repenting. Only after three rounds with the prophet does Saul finally confess his true motive.

> "'I violated the Lord's command and your instructions. I was afraid of the men, and so I gave in to them. Now I beg you, forgive my sin and come back with me, so that I may worship the Lord.'
>
> But Samuel said to him, 'I will not go back with you. You have rejected the word of the Lord, and the Lord has rejected you as king over Israel!' As Samuel turned to leave, Saul caught hold of the hem of his robe, and it tore. Samuel said to him, 'The Lord has torn the kingdom of Israel from you today and has given it to one of your neighbors—to one better than you. He who is the Glory of Israel does not lie or change his mind; for he is not a human being, that he should change his mind'" (1 Sam 15:24–29).

In the last chapter we witnessed Samson's similar failure to lead in faithfulness. He wrestled with a different type of sin but encountered the same outcome. It quenched the Spirit's power in his life. Whereas Samson sought restoration and sacrificed his final breaths in a heroic triumph of justice, however, Saul finished out his days steeped in his dark side.

Blind to the driving insecurities within, Saul chased the elusive approval of others while living in relational isolation. He viewed everyone around him as a threat, wielding his authority as a weapon to control and manipulate. Suspicious even of his own flesh and blood, his conflicted soul manifested itself in increasingly paranoid behaviors. The king who rose from humble beginnings, empowered by the Spirit to lead God's people, withdrew into a shell of the man he could have been. He never moved forward from his failures, and the final scene of his life played out on the battlefield where he fell on his own sword.

Saul the people-pleaser fought his whole life for a sense of security. He feared his family's response to Samuel's anointing. He feared the constituents who questioned his worthiness of kingship. He feared his soldiers lest they distrust and abandon him, and he feared his own son, lest he outshine him. Saul died never knowing the peace that awaited him in true partnership with the Spirit. Unwilling to trust beyond what he could see, Saul's persistent disobedience prevented him from attaining what he desired most, the security and significance realized in a relationship with the God who called him.

Every personality has its own dysfunctional tendencies. Some of us are prone to people-pleasing, others wrestle with pride or lust or anger. Just as we discovered in Samson's story, Saul's encounter with the Spirit emphasizes his willingness to partner with imperfect people. Clothed by the Spirit, Saul fought bravely for the safety of Israel, but he continually set his compass by the fickle opinions of men rather than trusting the faithfulness of God. Eventually, the whole kingdom suffered for it.

> "The mind governed by the flesh is death, but the mind governed by the Spirit is life and peace" (Rom 8: 6).

Torn between pleasing God and securing the approval of men, Saul lived a conflicted man. He experienced relational death within his family because he couldn't see past his threatened ego. He suffered spiritual death by quenching the Spirit, and he eventually reaped physical death by taking his own life. His mind, governed by the flesh, led him to places of defeat and despair, places void of peace.

I may always feel the pull of my people-pleasing nature, but I can still experience the peace of one whose mind is governed by the Spirit. You can, too. It all hinges on who we submit to. If we relinquish our will to the opinions of others, we'll encounter a fate similar to Saul's. Always on guard, isolated in our distrust and suspicions, we'll reap relational and spiritual death. As we surrender to the Spirit, however, we reap life. We reap peace. He is source of security we seek, and we can trust him without doubt or fear.

DIGGING DEEPER:

- Saul deflected Samuel's warnings by defending himself. How do you usually respond to criticism?

- We all have room to grow in this area! What might growth look like in your natural reactions?

- Saul never moved beyond his failures because he rationalized his choices instead of repenting. How can we protect ourselves from falling into this habit?

- The author writes, "Setting our course to the erratic sway of popular opinion renders us ineffective and forces us to prioritize the approval of others above God." In what ways might it render us ineffective?

- How does a connection with the Spirit counteract the dangers of people-pleasing?

- This chapter revealed the Spirit as the Source of peace. How does knowing this aspect of his personality encourage you to trust him more? And how might that trust transform your life?

Chapter Nine

David and the Hope of the Fallen

1 Samuel 16—2 Samuel 23

In Dicken's classic Christmas tale, a visiting spirit grants a penny-pinching miser a foreboding glimpse of his future. The man awakens from the vision inspired to change his ways and secure a happier fate than the one portrayed. Filmmakers periodically reinvent variations of this traditional tale where someone wakes up in an alternate reality, a version of their life in which they made a different choice at some pinnacle moment in their past. Before the movie finishes, the main character finds a chance at redemption, and as the credits roll we catch a sneak peak of their now more wonderful life.

I wonder how differently Saul's legacy would look if he encountered such a vision and determined to trust the Spirit rather than anchor his security in the approval of others. I doubt the king imagined a future version of himself so paranoid, so consumed by insecurity that he used his own children as pawns in manipulative plots to garner loyalty, but that's who he became nonetheless. Perhaps a dream of the fate awaiting him would have inspired change and prevented that ugly spiral, but I suppose his denial of God's repeated warnings through the prophet Samuel suggests otherwise.

Saul never made the choice to change, but we do catch a glimpse of the legacy he could have left in the life of the one who succeeded him, King David. Despite being clothed by the same Spirit, the wayward soul of Saul and willing heart of David scripted very different stories. While Saul's story conveys a somber warning of sin's peril, David's offers the hopeful portrait of restoration made possible by repentance. Both kings wrestled with dark seasons of sin, but David sought forgiveness for his failures rather than rationalizing his rebellion like Saul. That single decision made all the difference in the legacy he left behind, a legacy in which the Spirit reveals himself as the Hope of the fallen.

David's first scene in Scripture follows the story we explored in the previous chapter when Samuel announced that God would tear the kingdom from Saul just like Saul tore the prophet's robe. Samuel left the battlefield grieving the king's self-inflicted fate until God told him to travel to the house of Jesse and anoint a new leader. The prophet obeyed at once and invited Jesse and his sons to a sacrifice. That's where we're first introduced to a young David.

> "Jesse had seven of his sons pass before Samuel, but Samuel said to him, 'The Lord has not chosen these.' So he asked Jesse, 'Are these all the sons you have?'
>
> 'There is still the youngest,' Jesse answered. 'He is tending the sheep.'
>
> Samuel said, 'Send for him; we will not sit down until he arrives.' So he sent for him and had him brought in. He was glowing with health and had a fine appearance and handsome features.
>
> Then the Lord said, 'Rise and anoint him; this is the one.' So Samuel took the horn of oil and anointed him in the presence of his brothers, and from that day on the Spirit of the Lord came powerfully upon David" (1 Sam 16:10–13).

Just as the Spirit came powerfully upon Samson and Saul, he now signifies God's presence with the newly anointed shepherd boy. Unlike Saul's more immediate ascent to the throne, David's road to royalty followed numerous detours. The intermingling of these two kings occurred in layers. David's first exposure to the monarchy came not as anointed heir but accomplished harpist. When the Spirit left Saul, Scripture says an evil spirit from the Lord tormented him. The servants recruited David to play his harp since music seemed to offer the king temporary relief from the mental anguish.

The term translated as "evil" in this passage is the Hebrew word *ra'*. Rather than intrinsic wickedness, it indicates an unpleasant or troubling nature. Anyone who has experienced devastating loss as a result of their own sinful choices will testify to the torment of regrets and what-ifs. The Spirit left Saul after he rejected the Lord; his rebellion led to this reality. He knew that he ruled on borrowed time and only had himself to blame for it. Such an awareness troubled Saul in the deepest, darkest corners of his soul.

> "Whenever the spirit from God came on Saul, David would take up his lyre and play. Then relief would come to Saul he would feel better, and the evil spirit would leave him" (1 Sam 16:23).

The irony of this image speaks volumes. The anguished king finds rare moments of peace in the presence of the heir chosen to replace him, the one clothed by the very same Spirit Saul rejected. Over the years the paradox of this picture has inspired countless artists to capture the scene on canvas. A quick online image search reveals various motifs portraying a downcast Saul hunched over the throne with head in hand while David plays his harp with face turned upward as if towards heaven. The subtle posturing of both characters contrasts the defeat of one king with the devotion of the other. Once again the truth of Romans 8:6 rings true: "The mind governed by the flesh is death, but the mind governed by the Spirit is life and peace."

If ever two men personified this verse it would be Saul and David in this moment—the tortured king who followed fleshly desires for human approval down a path of self-destruction versus the serenity of a simple shepherd boy who pursued the Spirit and radiated his life-giving peace. The Bible doesn't indicate how many months or years David played music to calm the war raging within Saul, but we know that the two later interacted on a different sort of battlefield. The palace musician traded his harp for a slingshot and aided the king in a fight against the Philistines.

> "Now the Philistines gathered their forces for war and assembled at Sokoh in Judah. They pitched camp at Ephes Dammim, between Sokoh and Azekah. Saul and the Israelites assembled and camped in the Valley of Elah and drew up their battle line to meet the Philistines" (1 Sam 17:1–2).

The heroic showdown between David and Goliath is one of the Old Testament's most infamous and inspiring stories. A shepherd boy with five stones and a slingshot faces off against a giant clad in bronze armor with a sword of iron and somehow, against all odds, he wins. Saul takes note of the brave young man only to realize it is David, son of Jesse, who once played the harp for him.

Scholars question why Saul did not recognize him sooner. Some suggest the difference in context as one possible reason. During his time as a harpist, David traveled back and forth between the royal residence and his home to care for his father's flock (1 Sam 17:15). He was not a permanent fixture at the palace, nor a prominent one. Saul lived surrounded by servants; the face of a boy behind a harp was probably not one he remembered, especially given the state of his sanity during that time. Following David's heroics on the battlefield, however, Saul took notice and enlisted him in full-time service. David joined the ranks of the royal fighting force, formed a deep friendship with Saul's son, Jonathon, and quickly earned the favor of the Israelite people.

> "David led the troops in their campaigns. In everything he did, he had great success, because the Lord was with him. When Saul saw how successful he was, he was afraid of him. But all Israel and Judah loved David because he led them in their campaigns" (1 Sam 18:13–16).

Recognizing the mark of a man empowered by the Spirit, Saul grew increasingly threatened by David. His paranoia erupted in multiple murder attempts and even the bait of marriage in hopes of manipulating his daughter to bring about David's downfall (1 Sam 18:11–21, 19:2–11). Eventually, Saul chased him into the wilderness where he lived like an outlaw.

From shepherd boy to royal musician to renegade, the detours of David's journey afforded ample opportunity for doubt and frustration, but he remained faithful. Banished from society, David, like Jephthah, formed a battalion of brothers willing to fight alongside him. Together they defended outlying towns still afflicted by the Philistine and Ammonite armies while surviving on the run from Saul's relentless pursuit.

Twice David encountered opportunities to ambush Saul easily; once he was close enough to cut the corner of the king's robe. His men encouraged him to take advantage of the moment and kill the competition, but David trusted the Lord's timing. Even after Saul fell on his sword, the wait for the throne continued as Saul's son made a play for the position, and conflict ensued (2 Sam 3:1).

Despite years of difficulty and disappointment, David experienced the peace of one who entrusted his storyline to the Spirit's lead. However, when God fulfilled his promise to David, and he finally ruled over Israel as King, temptation ensnared him by way of a beautiful woman named Bathsheba. After seeing her bathing on a rooftop, David brought her to his house and slept with her. When she sent news of her unexpected pregnancy, David created a ruse to solve the problem. He called her husband, Uriah, home from the battlefield in hopes the soldier would sleep with his wife and assume the child born just shy of nine months later was his own flesh and blood. The honorable man refused to sleep anywhere but the king's doorstep, however, as a sign of solidarity with his fellow warriors still fighting on the front lines. David repaid the soldier's allegiance with disloyalty of the worst kind. He sent Uriah back to the battlefield carrying his own death sentence in the form of a note to the commanding officer (2 Sam 11:1–17).

Adultery.

Conspiracy.

Murder.

Such depravity defiled David's formerly faithful legacy. His sin rivaled Saul's and similarly jeopardized his partnership with the Spirit. Whereas Saul rejected God's reprimand, however, David listened. When the prophet Nathan used the parable of a poor man's lamb to convict the king of his sin, it inspired the following prayer of repentance:

> "Have mercy on me, O God, according to your unfailing love; according to your great compassion blot out my transgressions. Wash away all my iniquity and cleanse me from my sin. Create in me a pure heart, O God, and renew a steadfast spirit within me. Do not cast me from your presence or take your Holy Spirit from me. Restore to me the joy of your salvation and grant me a willing spirit, to sustain me" (Ps 51:1–2, 10–12).

David knew that the Spirit would not reside where sin reigned. He saw his fate in flashbacks to the early days when he played his harp for a troubled king and ushered in the only peace Saul could find. David witnessed the torment of a soul haunted by the loss of the Spirit, and he begged God for a second chance. He pleaded for the Spirit to stay present with him.

David knew the hope made possible in the Spirit, and he clung to it. Before he ascended the throne, he'd experienced its sustaining power as he waited for God to fulfill his promise. Despite persecution, starvation, and years spent living on the run as Saul's army chased him without just cause, David faithfully waited. He didn't cave to peer pressure. He didn't yield to the impatience of his own heart. He didn't surrender to despair despite scenarios suggesting God had forgotten all about him. He waited with a hope that did not disappoint.

God responded to David's repentant plea with a grace-filled pardon. His sin carried consequences, but forgiveness enabled full fellowship with the Spirit again. Whereas Saul's life ended in defeat on the battlefield, David's closing scene played out against a backdrop of peace. His final breaths expressed hopeful assurances of restoration he attributed to the Spirit.

"The Spirit of the Lord spoke through me; his word was on my tongue. The God of Israel spoke, the Rock of Israel said to me: 'When one rules over people in righteousness, when he rules in the fear of God, he is like the light of morning at sunrise on a cloudless morning, like the brightness after rain that brings grass from the earth.' If my house were not right with God, surely he would not have made with me an everlasting covenant, arranged and secured in every part" (2 Sam 23:2–5).

David's fall did not define his legacy. Despite the folly of adultery and foulness of murder, he found the forgiveness he needed to move forward from his failure and fulfill his purpose as a king after God's own heart. The Spirit empowered his restoration, and David finished his days ruling in righteousness.

Such is the redemptive hope of the Spirit. He enables victory in perhaps the most difficult arena of all, the battlefield of the human heart. Saul and David both failed in their leadership roles, but David did not allow his fall to cripple his future. He lived, and died, assured that his house stood right before the Lord.

Like the kings of ancient Israel, we face temptation. We sin, and our sin comes at a cost, but we can choose whose example we follow in the aftermath. If we respond like Saul, justifying our choices and quenching the Spirit rather than admitting our wrong, we'll share his fate. If you want more for your future than the anguish of regrets, remember David. Reflect on his story. The same Spirit that restored David offers redemption to all who repent. His presence ushers in the peace of forgiveness that enables us to fulfill our purpose in God's Kingdom. We may fail, but we can count on the Spirit, the Hope of the fallen, to fashion a means of restoration.

"May the God of hope fill you with all joy and peace as you trust in him, so that you may overflow with hope by the power of the Holy Spirit" (Rom 15:13).

DIGGING DEEPER:

- What can you learn from a comparison of Saul and David?

- We've clearly seen the Spirit's heart for redemption. Why might someone struggle to embrace the hope of restoration after they've failed?

- How can this aspect of the Spirit's personality help us rebuild relationships with people who have broken our trust?

- How could God call a king guilty of adultery, conspiracy, and murder a "man after his own heart"?

- This chapter revealed the Spirit as the Hope of the fallen. How does knowing this aspect of his personality encourage you to trust him more? And how might that trust transform your life?

Chapter Ten

Elijah and the Mover of Men

1 Kings 18:1–12

Just before our family moved across the ocean to the mission field of Papua New Guinea, we rented a little house by the railroad tracks. A fixer-upper for sure, it wasn't much to brag about. The backyard was more gravel than grass when we first moved in, but it had a perfect little climbing tree right next to a cement pad that spawned all sorts of imaginary play. My younger brother and I used to pretend that we were ninja warriors who teleported from our spaceship to the landing pad just in time to save the day. We made our own sound effects, performed all of our own stunts, and succeeded at being the best little ninjas our Midwestern town had ever seen.

I haven't beamed my way down from any trees lately, and as a general rule I leave topics like teleportation to the science fiction writers and stick with theology. For this next encounter between the Holy Spirit and humankind, however, the two genres collide in a mysterious way. Even though we've discovered a deeper appreciation for who the Spirit is and why knowing him matters, there are still elements of his nature veiled in mystery, aspects we aren't quite able to wrap our minds around, such as the one we're about to discover.

Lest we read tales of men like Moses and Gideon—who faced agonizing fears to accomplish astonishing feats—and reduce the Spirit to some sort of psychological philosophy, Elijah's experience reveals a Spirit who is not so easily boxed in. The Spirit is more than a therapeutic cure for insecurities or extra burst of bravery in battle. He is God. Almighty, all-powerful, awe-inspiring God! He's a supernatural phenomenon, and his partnership with the prophet Elijah is unlike any encounter we've explored thus far.

Elijah first enters the scene during the reign of King Ahab, a wicked ruler with an evil wife, Jezebel. During a season of spiritual harlotry, Elijah encouraged the wayward Israelites towards faithfulness. You may recall a few of his more infamous stories in Scripture such as the time he repaid a widow's kindness by prophesying that her flour and oil would not run dry until the drought ended. Or perhaps you remember when Elijah outran the King's chariot or prayed for the restoration of life to a little boy. Probably his most well-known story is when he challenged the prophets of Baal to a duel, and God sent fire from heaven to consume Elijah's offering and confirm his commanding presence (1 Kgs 17:7—18:45).

Of all the wonders God empowered Elijah to accomplish, Scripture specifically links the Spirit to only one, the miraculous movement from one location to another. Multiple people at various times in the prophet's life anticipated that the Spirit would transport Elijah from their presence to a different place such as a nearby town or somewhere in the mountains. Hence the reason why this chapter triggered childhood memories of imaginary teleportation from our backyard tree!

The first reference to this unusual aspect of Elijah's partnership with the Spirit coincides with a chance meeting between the prophet and the palace administrator out in the countryside. Past run-ins with the royal couple created a sense of hostility between Elijah and the king, but Ahab's administrator, Obadiah, was a God-follower. In fact, when Queen Jezebel went on a killing spree against Yahweh's prophets, Obadiah hid many of them in caves, providing safety and provisions unbeknownst to his employers.

When Elijah crossed paths with the Obadiah, he asked him to alert Ahab of his presence so that he might seek an audience with the king. The royal official bowed low to the ground in recognition of the man of God before him but resisted Elijah's request saying, "I don't know where the Spirit of the Lord may carry you when I leave you. If I go and tell Ahab and he doesn't find you, he will kill me" (1 Kgs 18:12).

Although prior passages in Scripture do not explain when or why or how, apparently Elijah had developed a reputation for disappearing. It occurred often enough that even a palace administrator expected it and embraced it as a mark of the Spirit's divine presence with Elijah. Though Obadiah was a devout believer in Yahweh, this particular expression of supernatural power could cause him a lot of trouble. He feared that the Spirit would carry Elijah away before he came back with Ahab, and he knew if that happened that the King would accuse him of lying and sentence him to death.

The Hebrew word translated here as "carrying" is the term *nasa*. The word occurs nearly six hundred times in Scripture, sometimes in a literal context and sometimes used figuratively. For example, men were told to lift up *(nasa)* their hands to take an oath, as a way of signaling, or when carrying out acts of punishment.[1] Figurative uses include the lifting *(nasa)* of one's head as a restoration to honor, the lifting of one's emotions, or the carrying away of sin.[2]

Since the term itself can be literal or figurative depending on the context, how do we determine the intended use of this particular passage? Maybe Obadiah did not expect a literal, physical carrying away of the prophet after all. Perhaps he implied a figurative carrying in the sense that the Spirit moved Elijah via an internal prompting to leave one area and travel to another. Such an understanding certainly eases the tension of explaining Spirit-powered

---

1. Deut 32:40; Ezk 20:5; Isa 49:22; 2 Sam 18:28; Ps 10:12
2. Gen 40:13; Job 10:15; Exod 34:7; Num 14:18; Mic 7:18

teleportation. I confess it's easier to believe in a figurative carrying than one that breaks the laws of physics and breaches human rationale, but before we determine how to best interpret the *nasa* of the Spirit in Elijah's life, we should address a second reference to this reputation for disappearing.

Several years after this encounter with King Ahab's palace administrator, Elijah met and mentored his replacement, Elisha. After a season of shared ministry between the two, God carried the aging prophet away to heaven. When Elisha told the others about Elijah's death, they refused to accept it. Convinced he must still be alive, fifty men spread out to search for him saying, "Perhaps the Spirit of the Lord has picked him up *(nasa)* and set him down on some mountain or in some valley" (2 Kgs 2:16).

Far less ambiguous, this instance combines an active carrying with the eventual putting back down. The men believed no-one could find Elijah because the Spirit had deposited him on a mountain or in a valley. If they merely searched the area, they were bound to see him. It was easier for them to believe this than to accept that the prophet had indeed died.

Other instances of divine teleportation in Scripture can further help inform our interpretation of Elijah's unconventional partnership with the Spirit. Oddly enough, he was not the only biblical hero who experienced this miraculous movement. Consider the following story from the New Testament about Philip, a disciple of Jesus.

> "Now an angel of the Lord said to Philip, 'Go south to the road—the desert road—that goes down from Jerusalem to Gaza.' So he started out, and on his way, he met an Ethiopian eunuch, an important official in charge of all the treasury of the Kandake (which means "queen of the Ethiopians"). This man had gone to Jerusalem to worship, and on his way home was sitting in his chariot reading the Book of Isaiah the prophet. The Spirit told Philip, 'Go to that chariot and stay near it.' Then Philip ran up to the chariot and heard the man reading Isaiah the prophet.

'Do you understand what you are reading?' Philip asked. Philip began with that very passage of Scripture and told him the good news about Jesus.

As they traveled along the road, they came to some water, and the eunuch said, 'Look, here is water. What can stand in the way of my being baptized?' And he gave orders to stop the chariot. Then both Philip and the eunuch went down into the water, and Philip baptized him. When they came up out of the water, the Spirit of the Lord suddenly took Philip away, and the eunuch did not see him again but went on his way rejoicing. Philip, however, appeared at Azotus and traveled about, preaching the gospel in all the towns until he reached Caesarea" (Acts 8:26–30, 35–40).

This New Testament narrative helps us understand Elijah's story in two ways. First, it reveals that if God moves someone via a voice from heaven or an internal prompting to leave and go somewhere else, Scripture phrases it as such. The angel of the Lord told Philip to go near the chariot, and Philip did so without any supernatural flair; he simply ran on his own two legs.

Secondly, it reinforces a literal interpretation through a difference in terminology between how the Spirit moved Philip and how Philip moved himself. The verb used for the Spirit carrying him away is *harpazo*, a Greek derivative of the same Hebrew term used in both passages regarding Elijah. It can also translate as "snatched away" and conveys a sudden and forceful action by the Spirit. Philip is carried away *(harpazo)* from the Ethiopian and appears *(heurisko)*[3] in Azotus, a city several miles northwest. He is not the originator of the action but rather a passive recipient. In a sense, he was merely along for the ride. After appearing there, however, he travels *(dierchomai)*[4] of his own accord towards Caesarea.

I include the Greek terminology to clarify the difference in movement between the beginning and end of the narrative. At the start when he ran toward the eunuch and again at the very end

3. Greek verb *heurisko*—*"found himself"*
4. Greek verb *dierchomai*—*"pass through; journey"*

when he traveled towards Caesarea, Philip is the originator of the movement. In the middle, however, the Spirit is the active mover. He carries Philip away from the southern road to Gaza, and then the disciple appears in the town of Azotus.

The linguistic and contextual elements emphasize a literal transportation from one place to another by the supernatural power of the Spirit. Whether we call it teleportation or something a little more sacred sounding like miraculous movement, religious re-routing, divine displacement or a blessed beaming, we're talking about something physical. Although there are places in Scripture when the Spirit carries a person via a vision or dream, those experiences are described as such.

For example, Ezekiel was caught up by the Spirit "in a vision" several times.[5] In the New Testament, people like Paul and John also encountered visions by way of the Spirit to reveal prophecy or truth.[6] Elijah's experience, however, is not described as a vision. Men who knew him and his reputation expected that when his body vanished from view, they could go and find him physically present somewhere else. It was not metaphorical or metaphysical but a literal movement of matter from one location to another.

I do not pretend to understand the physics of such a feat, nor am I entirely sure of its purpose. Perhaps God wanted to draw attention to Elijah as a prophet who was supernaturally empowered by the Spirit. Such a unique reputation would undoubtedly accomplish widespread awareness. Maybe it was merely a matter of convenience; perhaps Elijah was needed in another place faster than typical human travel could accomplish. All in all, I have more questions than answers about Elijah's unconventional partnership with the Spirit. This chapter of his story again illustrates why we often struggle to connect with him as easily as we do God the Father or Christ the Son. He's different, and in cases like this one, different is difficult to wrap our minds around.

The Spirit's complex nature does not negate the insights gained in this chapter, however. Though the eccentricity of his

5. Ezek 3:12, 14; 8:3; 11:1, 24; 43:5
6. 2 Cor 12:2; Rev 1:9–16

unique partnership with Elijah may elicit feelings of confusion or discomfort, it reveals an exciting aspect of his character that we would otherwise miss. He is a miraculous mover of men, and that peculiar piece of his personality matters because we live in a world that doesn't always follow predictable patterns.

As much as we want life to move along in ways that make sense to us, it doesn't. Life rarely fits nice and tidy into the box we wish it did. Unexpected tragedies pull the rug out from under us in devastating ways. Obstacles we didn't foresee can rise before us like unmovable mountains. We can wake up to our usual routine one morning and face an impossible reality the next. Your phone could ring this very moment with news that will forever change your life.

I'm not trying to be dramatic; I'm speaking from experience. Maybe you've lived through that type of phone call already. If not, you probably know someone who has. A heart attack, a house fire, financial collapse or family betrayal. Life ceases to make sense in these kinds of moments. That's when we need a Spirit who supersedes human understanding, a Spirit who busts out of the little box we're tempted to put him in and reminds us that nothing, absolutely nothing, is impossible for him.

> "I pray that out of his glorious riches he may strengthen you with power through his Spirit in your inner being. Now to him who is able to do immeasurably more than all we ask or imagine, according to his power that is at work within us, to him be glory in the church and in Christ Jesus throughout all generations, for ever and ever! Amen" (Eph 3:16, 20–21).

Elijah's story reveals a Spirit who is able to do immeasurably more than anything we could ask or imagine. He created the laws of physics, and he can break every rule in the book if he sees fit. He can move men from place to place just because he's that mind-blowingly powerful. This mysterious merging of science-fiction and theology may be weird, but it's weirdly wonderful!

When we're faced with the unthinkable, the unbelievable, and we can't find a way through, we know one who can. We can lean on the Spirit of unlimited strength, a Spirit big enough to work in ways our finite minds cannot comprehend. We can trust the one capable of moving men and moving mountains.

DIGGING DEEPER:

- Reflect on a time when life veered from the route you expected. How might this "out of the box" aspect of the Spirit's personality encourage someone in a similar situation?

- How do the experiences of others like Philip help inform your interpretation of Elijah's unconventional partnership with the Spirit?

- "This mysterious merging of science-fiction and theology may be weird, but it's weirdly wonderful!" How do you feel about this peculiar chapter of the Spirit's study?

- How would you respond to someone who opted to ignore this reference to the Spirit rather than wrestle with how odd it seems?

- This chapter revealed the Spirit as a miraculous mover of men. How does knowing this aspect of his personality encourage you to trust him more? And how might that trust transform your life?

Chapter Eleven

***

Prophets, Kings, and the Voice of Truth

2 Chronicles 15–20

Truth. Sometimes it's hard to speak, hard to hear, and harder still to accept. Ever since Adam and Eve fell for Satan's deception and tried to cover it up with fig leaves and finger-pointing, humankind has struggled with issues of honesty. We've learned to live in a world of grey, smudging the line between black and white to suit our selfish preferences. We lie to please ourselves, and we lie to protect ourselves. In all the years since Eden's apple, we've yet to outgrow this habit of twisting the truth.

The temptation to deceive surfaces early on in life, and we finesse the art of fibbing as we age. When we're little, our lies often reveal the very thing we're trying to conceal. For example, my husband and I once caught our foster-daughter with chocolate smudges from fingertips to elbows and all around her mouth. She could have won awards for her performance that night, acting as surprised as we were to discover the mysterious chocolate on her arms and face. She couldn't fathom where it came from, but she was quick to point out that it was definitely *not* the leftover pudding from the fridge!

As humorous as some of those childish lies can be, they highlight the human tendency of avoiding truth rather than admitting it. When sin entangles itself in our life, it pulls us towards places of darkness and isolation. We hide, just like Adam and Eve hid from God in the garden and our pudding-covered little girl avoided us. In this particular chapter of the Spirit's story, he reveals himself as the Voice of truth who draws the wayward out of hiding and into the light of restored relationships. He reminds us to walk righteously in full fellowship with God, taking every step forward in the love and freedom he lavishes upon all who accept him.

As noted earlier, however, we don't always want to accept the truth. God's people have a long history of closing their ears to the Spirit's voice. Israel habitually rejected his words to justify their worship of foreign gods. Their spiritual harlotry cycled for centuries, spanning from the time of the judges through the time of the kings and beyond. When the Spirit inspired prophets to voice his truth, the people refused to listen and further damaged their relationship with God. Only when the consequences of their sin proved too heavy a burden to bear did Israel respond to his words and repent of their ways.

We witnessed this cycle with Othniel, Gideon, and Samson. By the time David's grandson assumed the throne, the once unified Israelite nation had split into two idolatrous kingdoms. Jeroboam ruled over the larger portion in the north and Rehoboam reigned over the southern country called Judah. Both kings did evil in the eyes of the Lord, as did their heirs. Even so, the Spirit continued partnering with prophets to speak light into sin's darkness. One such prophet, Azariah, went to King Asa, a more willing listener than his disobedient forefathers. His two-fold message promised favor to the faithful and warned against the folly of forsaking God.

> "The Spirit of God came upon Azariah the son of Oded, and he went out to meet Asa and said to him, 'Hear me, Asa, and all Judah and Benjamin: The Lord is with you while you are with him. If you seek him, he will be found by you, but if you forsake him, he will forsake you'" (2 Chr 15:1–2).

Despite inheriting a land rampant with idolatry and rebellion, Asa demonstrated a desire for a more devout reign. He sought to rectify the waywardness of the royal family by purging the land of idols, expelling male shrine prostitutes, and restoring a sense of holiness to Israelite worship. The Spirit knew time had a way of dwindling devotion, however, so he dispatched Azariah with this clear-cut decree.

Notice that King Asa did not initiate this exchange or authorize the prophet's approach. Azariah invited himself to an impromptu audience with the king, a bold but risky move. He spoke the Spirit's truth without asking for permission and risked a potentially dangerous reaction. If Asa viewed the statement as an assumption on Azariah's part that the king was already slipping in his devotion or guilty of some secret sin warranting the public admonition, he could have punished the prophet for his presumptuous correction of royalty. Fortunately for the prophet and the Israelite people, however, Asa welcomed the word of truth. He listened to the Spirit and responded with a grand display of communal devotion. He gathered the people together at Jerusalem to renew their covenant with God.

> "All Judah rejoiced about the oath because they had sworn it wholeheartedly. They sought God eagerly, and he was found by them. So the Lord gave them rest on every side" (2 Chr 15:15).

As a result of their faithfulness, God granted Judah a season of national peace. Their countrymen in the Northern Kingdom, however, remained unwilling to heed God's warnings. Enemy pressure plagued them for several years, and eventually, King Ahab, whom we met in the previous chapter, reached out to Asa's heir, King Jehoshaphat for assistance in battle. He asked Judah's king to aid Northern Israel against their enemies, but Jehoshaphat encouraged Ahab to inquire of God's will in the matter first.

Having severed his connection with Yahweh through years of idol worship and the persecution of truth-telling prophets like Elijah, Ahab obliged with a false display of faith. He gathered four hundred prophets from among Israel, each one willing to say exactly what they knew their king wanted to hear. Accustomed to "divining" prophetic words designed to please the king, all four hundred affirmed Ahab's battle plans and promised rousing success.

Jehoshaphat did not fall for the charade, however. He recognized the difference between a phony prophet who only spoke favorably and one marked by the Spirit of God who spoke the truth regardless of the recipient's response. Ahab finally admitted, "There is still one prophet through whom we can inquire of the Lord, but I hate him because he never prophesies anything good about me, but always bad. He is Micaiah son of Imlah" (2 Chr 18:7).

This brings us to a second vital partnership between the Spirit and a prophet appointed to voice his truth in the era of ancient kings. Micaiah already knew from past experiences that King Ahab despised him, but he remained a willing vessel amidst a sea of false prophets. Though he stood as the single naysayer against the combined chorus of four hundred others, and though the king would hate him all the more for it, Micaiah spoke the Spirit's truth precisely as it was entrusted to him.

He told the king that his prophets were merely deceiving spirits sent to entice him. The victory they promised was nothing more than a foolish illusion spun to appease. Rather than absolute success, Micaiah prophesied an outcome from the battle that would leave Israel scattered like sheep without a shepherd for "the Lord has decreed disaster for you" (2 Chr 18:22). Upon hearing these words, the king's supporters reprimanded Micaiah's insolence and slapped him in the face. Ahab threw the prophet in prison with strict instructions to feed him nothing but bread and water until he returned from war.

As noted at the beginning of this chapter, truth is hard to speak, hard to hear, and harder still to accept. Micaiah bravely voiced truth, but Ahab refused to listen. He rejected the Spirit's warning, went to war, and perished from the random arrow of an enemy archer. The arrow lodged itself perfectly between two pieces of armor, an improbable injury reflective of the holes in Ahab's flawed battle plan. His decision to reject the Spirit's truth and trust the strategy of men instead resulted in fatal defeat.

Both Azariah and Micaiah obeyed the Spirit's call to speak the truth. Both Asa and Ahab had the opportunity to hear and accept that truth. One did, and one died. King Asa received the truth and enjoyed peace, but Ahab's defiance led to his downfall.

The Spirit's truth never fails. If he calls us to speak the truth, we must voice the message entrusted to us. If he calls us to hear the truth, we must be willing to listen.

And then we must believe.

Accepting the Spirit's truth when our eyes and mind see things differently stretches our faith. It makes his word difficult to receive, but Ahab's example warns against trusting our own vision over his voice. When King Jehoshaphat later faced an impending attack against Judah, he had the chance to follow his own advice and seek the Lord's will in the matter. The Spirit responded by raising a third prophet to voice his truth, a descendant of the Levitical musicians.

> "The Spirit of the Lord came on Jahaziel son of Zechariah, the son of Benaiah, the son of Jeiel, the son of Mattaniah, a Levite and descendant of Asaph, as he stood in the assembly. He said: 'Listen, King Jehoshaphat and all who live in Judah and Jerusalem! This is what the Lord says to you: 'Do not be afraid or discouraged because of this vast army. For the battle is not yours, but God's. Tomorrow march down against them. They will be climbing up by the Pass of Ziz, and you will find them at the end of the gorge in the Desert of Jeruel. You will not have to fight this battle. Take up your positions; stand firm and see the deliverance the Lord will give you'" (2 Chr 20:14–17).

Amidst the threat of war, the Spirit spoke a message hard to hear, and harder still to accept. His unconventional battle plan called for Jehoshaphat to prepare the troops, take up position, and then pause. Approach, but do not fight. Draw near, but don't engage.

Wait.

Watch.

And surely the Lord would deliver them.

Such a strategy tested the king's faith. Jehoshaphat felt the full weight of every man, woman, and child whose lives depended on his decision. With armies already amassed against them, the plan to wait and watch made little sense. Even so, Judah's king chose to trust the Spirit and obey. He promised to lead his warriors to the brink of the battlefield and wait, just as the Spirit instructed.

The story plays out in 2 Chronicles 20:18–29. Jehoshaphat and his troops move forward in faith, and the king assigns men from the front to lead the soldiers in songs of praise. Unbeknownst to the singing Israelites, God was already ambushing their adversaries. Their enemies turned on one another, and before one of Jehoshaphat's warriors could lift a finger, the fight was finished, the battle won.

> "When the men of Judah came to the place that overlooks the desert and looked toward the vast army, they saw only dead bodies lying on the ground; no one had escaped. Then, led by Jehoshaphat, all the men of Judah and Jerusalem returned joyfully to Jerusalem, for the Lord had given them cause to rejoice over their enemies. They entered Jerusalem and went to the temple of the Lord with harps and lyres and trumpets. The fear of God came on all the surrounding kingdoms when they heard how the Lord had fought against the enemies of Israel" (2 Chr 20:24, 27–29).

Sometimes truth is hard to speak. Sometimes it's hard to hear and harder still to believe, but the Spirit's truth is always trustworthy. He sent Azariah to remind Asa to keep seeking the Lord, and Asa's acceptance of truth ushered in a several-year stretch of peace for Judah. The Spirit sent Micaiah to warn Ahab, but the king rejected his message, failing the northern nation and forfeiting his own life. He rose up yet another prophet, Jahaziel, to voice an impossible battle plan to King Jehoshaphat, and Jehoshaphat's obedience to the word wrought victory.

Some leaders listened, and others hardened their hearts against him, but the Spirit refused to let his people stumble in darkness for lack of knowledge. His word led the willing followers like a lamp unto their feet and a light unto their path (Ps 119:105). He valued his relationship with them enough to continue raising up vessels to voice his truth whether the people believed his message or not.

The same Spirit who voiced truth amidst impending battle in Old Testament times encourages faithful God-followers to stand firm against the enemy who "prowls around like a roaring lion looking for someone to devour" (1 Pet 5:8). Satan, the father of lies, knows that deception will disconnect us from our source of life in God, and he masquerades as an angel of light to tempt us towards darkness. Our enemy is real. Our battle is real, but so is our victory if we're willing to listen and live by the Spirit's truth.

> "For our struggle is not against flesh and blood, but against the rulers, against the authorities, against the powers of this dark world and the spiritual forces of evil in the heavenly realms. Therefore, put on the full armor of God, so that when the day of evil comes, you may be able to stand your ground, and after you have done everything, to stand. Stand firm then, with the *belt of truth* buckled around your waist, with the breastplate of righteousness in place, and with your feet fitted with the readiness that comes from the gospel of peace. In addition to all this, take up the shield of faith, with which you can extinguish all the flaming arrows of the evil one. Take the helmet of salvation and the *sword of the Spirit*, which is the word of God" (Eph 6:12–17; *emphasis mine*).

As we wage spiritual war on behalf of God's kingdom today, we must do so with the belt of truth firmly in place. For ancient soldiers, a fastened belt signified readiness for battle. It steadied both the upper and lower armor and carried the weight of the attached sword. Without it, a soldier entered the field ill-equipped to protect himself and fight his enemy.

We defend ourselves against the depravity of this world with the sword of the Spirit, the word of God. His word is illuminating truth that pierces sin-saturated darkness like a double-edged sword. It comforts, it convicts, and it enables us to see what is right and real in a world where false prophets spin and sell feel-good philosophies at alarming rates.

> "The word of God is alive and active. Sharper than any double-edged sword, it penetrates even to dividing soul and spirit, joints and marrow; it judges the thoughts and attitudes of the heart" (Heb 4:12).

We need the Spirit's voice of truth in our lives. We need his comforting words of assurance when pressures threaten to overwhelm us and his conviction when we're tempted to turn a blind eye to sin. We are masters of self-deception, justifying what we know is wrong but struggle to change or let go of. It comes easily, and we can always find someone somewhere willing to agree with us. Ahab found four hundred prophets willing to back his battle plan, but their words were empty promises resulting in perilous outcomes.

The Spirit's priority is not to please but to protect. His truth guards our hearts against false promises that flatter for the moment but lead to places of darkness and death. Rather than fall victim to Satan's illusions, he wants us to live in the victory of real freedom. He loves us, and the light of his truth guides us so that we might fulfill our purpose in the kingdom without being ensnared by sin.

> "But when he, the Spirit of truth, comes, he will guide you into all the truth" (John 16:13).

> "It is the Spirit who testifies because the Spirit is the truth" (1 John 5:6).

Sometimes the Spirit's word is hard to speak, but we must be willing vessels to voice his truth, even if we're unsure how others will respond. Sometimes it's hard to hear, but we must remember that his truth is always trustworthy. We can accept it and move forward in faith knowing his word never fails.

We face a battle, but we do not face it alone. We are clothed with the Spirit, and our armor, unlike Ahab's, will protect against the arrows of the enemy. What the Spirit speaks, we can trust, for the Spirit *is* truth.

DIGGING DEEPER:

- The author suggests that sometimes "truth is hard to speak, hard to hear, and harder still to accept." When have you experienced this reality?

- Would you rather speak a difficult truth to someone or hear a difficult truth from someone? Why so?

- How would you distinguish between hearing truth and accepting it?

- Imagine you were one of these prophets. What concerns would you have about approaching the king with an unsolicited "truth bomb" from the Spirit?

- This chapter revealed the Spirit as the Voice of truth. How does knowing this aspect of his personality encourage you to trust him more? And how might that trust transform your life?

Chapter Twelve

Mary, Messiah, and the Spring of Life

Luke 1:26–35

I remember the night it happened. We were volunteering at the soup kitchen during the annual Christmas party, navigating narrow aisles to serve dinner and hand out colorfully packaged gifts. Sounds of the staff struggling to keep up in the kitchen mingled with the merriment of conversations around the tables. The crowded dining hall overflowed with happy chaos, so when my phone rang I slipped outside into the snowy silence to better hear.

That was the night my life forever changed.

My sister-in-law's voice echoed on the other end. Her announcement brought tears to my eyes, but not the sad kind. After we hung up, I lingered a little while longer, soaking in the quiet calm of gently falling flakes. I wanted to let the miracle marinate. After years of praying and waiting, our family was finally going to grow through the adventure of adoption.

Blessed with a beautiful teenage daughter through marriage and sweet baby boy through adoption, I'm grateful for every moment of motherhood. Of all the memories I cherish, however, that night remains a favorite. It inspired the name we gave our son, partly because the good news came during the Christmas season but mostly because his life was God's message to us that nothing was impossible for him. We named him Gabriel after the angel whose unexpected announcement conveyed a similar message to a young girl named Mary, the soon-to-be-mother of the Son of God.

> "God sent the angel Gabriel to Nazareth, a town in Galilee, to a virgin pledged to be married to a man named Joseph. 'Do not be afraid, Mary; you have found favor with God. You will conceive and give birth to a son, and you are to call him Jesus. He will be great and will be called the Son of the Most High. The Lord God will give him the throne of his father David, and he will reign over Jacob's descendants forever; his kingdom will never end.'
>
> 'How will this be,' Mary asked the angel, 'since I am a virgin?'
>
> The angel answered, 'The Holy Spirit will come on you, and the power of the Most High will overshadow you. So the holy one to be born will be called the Son of God'" (Luke 1:26, 30–35).

Like Gideon, Mary trusted the Author of impossible scripts to write a new narrative with her life, one she never expected but willingly embraced. The Spirit who created the world from an empty void stirred miraculous life within her virgin womb, and Mary gave birth to the Messiah. Though this particular partnership surfaces in the Gospels, it connects Old Testament prophecy with New Testament fulfillment revealing an overarching narrative from Genesis to Revelation. It brings the Spirit's story full circle, and so we'll breach our Old Testament borders to mine the riches buried in this final partnership when a young woman's life changed overnight with the promise of a son.

It should not surprise us to see the Spirit engaged in this pivotal moment of the Messiah's birth. After all, he's been a catalyst in every significant storyline transition thus far! He was there in the beginning, before the creation of the world, hovering over a worthless, watery wasteland. He drew forth potential and purpose from emptiness. Light pierced blackness and life began. The dry ground gave way to lush, green grass and fruit trees flowered in a kaleidoscope of color. Eden was paradise, and God enjoyed a complete connection with his creation. They walked and talked together in the garden until humankind rebelled and sin spoiled the scene.

In the wake of the fall, God expressed the depths of his love and mercy by penning a new narrative for the future. He promised that one day a Deliverer would forever free them from the consequences of evil and cleanse them from sin's stain. The Messiah would restore the severed relationship between Creator and creation in a completely new way through a sacrificial portrait of redemption. In the meantime, God chose Israel to shine like a light to the nations. The Spirit empowered Bezalel to build a tabernacle so that the Most High could again dwell among his people. He partnered with Moses and the seventy elders in cultivating a community to lead Israel in the united worship of the one, true God.

When rebellion infected the camp, and Israel suffered under enemy oppression, the Spirit empowered deliverance by clothing judges like Othniel, Gideon, and Samson. In partnership with the Spirit, these men embraced their role in the story, setting captive Israel free and administering justice to the enemy. In time the nation's leadership shifted from judges to kings, and the Spirit partnered with men like Saul and David to fight on Israel's behalf. When the kingdom faltered and idolatry found its way back into the Israelite community, the Spirit, the Voice of truth, partnered with prophets to speak words of wisdom and warning.

At every major twist and turn in God's redemptive plan, we see the Spirit alive and active. It only makes sense that he participates in the conception of Jesus Christ, the dawn of a new era in fulfillment of prophecy. The Spirit's partnership with Mary birthed his partnership with the Messiah, and their interlaced story reveals him as the Spring of life, the one who nurtures long-awaited promises to fruition.

> "A shoot will come up from the stump of Jesse;
> from his roots a Branch will bear fruit. The Spirit of
> the Lord will rest on him—the Spirit of wisdom and of

understanding, the Spirit of counsel and of might, the Spirit of the knowledge and fear of the Lord" (Isa 11:1–2).

This Messianic prophecy reveals a Spirit we've met before in the story of Bezalel, a Spirit of wisdom, understanding, and knowledge. As noted above, he partnered with Bezalel to build a dwelling place for God to reside among his people. Now God would reside with men in a whole new way.

"The Word became flesh and made his dwelling among us" (John 1: 14).

Jesus was no ordinary child, and as he grew Mary witnessed the angel Gabriel's prophesy come to life. Her precious boy was a portrait of God in person, walking among his people as one of them yet somehow still fully divine. Conceived by the Spirit through the power of the Most High, Christ was part of the original partnership, the Trinity. We capture a glimpse of the three-in-one together at Christ's baptism.

"As soon as Jesus was baptized, he went up out of the water. At that moment heaven was opened, and he saw the Spirit of God descending like a dove and alighting on him. And a voice from heaven said, 'This is my Son, whom I love; with him I am well pleased' (Matt 3:16–17).

Mary was not the only one who saw something special in Jesus. People flocked to him, and like a good shepherd he loved them. As public interest increased, he began to reveal his true nature as the Son of God. The gospel of Luke describes one particular Sabbath in Nazareth when he stood in front of the synagogue and read from the scroll of Isaiah.

"The Spirit of the Sovereign Lord is on me because the Lord has anointed me to proclaim good news to the poor. He has sent me to bind up the brokenhearted, to proclaim freedom for the captives and release from darkness for the prisoners" (Isa 61:1).

After reading the prophecy, Jesus proclaimed to the gathered crowd, "Today this Scripture is fulfilled in your hearing" (Luke 4:21). He affirmed his partnership with the Spirit whose power described in these verses matches the person we've already discovered in Old Testament partnerships. The Spirit revealed himself as the binder of the brokenhearted through his partnership with Jephthah, the rejected son of a harlot whose wounds found healing in his redemptive touch. He proclaimed freedom for the captives through His collaboration with Israelite judges and kings who defeated their enemies in miraculous ways. He illuminated darkness as the Voice of truth, speaking through prophets like Azariah, Micaiah, and Jahaziel to warn people against sin's enslavement. The Spirit's partnership with the Messiah is not a new collaboration after all but a culmination of everything we've uncovered about his trustworthy character thus far.

> "Jesus stood and said in a loud voice, 'Let anyone who is thirsty come to me and drink. Whoever believes in me, as Scripture has said, rivers of living water will flow from within them.' By this he meant the Spirit" (John 7:37–39).

From creation of the world to conception of the Savior, he is the source and sustainer of life. He sustained Israel's physical life as the Champion of second chances and just Deliverer. He sustained the relational fabric of the people as the Cultivator of community. He sustained their spiritual life as the Voice of truth who pointed them back towards God.

We live in a world that so quickly drains us dry. Busy schedules overwhelm our families, cripple our churches, and foster a sense of isolation so profound it endangers the well-being of our souls. We wrestle through lonely wilderness seasons where weariness becomes the new standard and vitality slowly withers away. We crave more than this perpetual physical, relational, and spiritual fatigue. We thirst for the life-giving waters of the Spirit.

> "The Spirit is poured on us from on high, and the desert becomes a fertile field, and the fertile field seems like a forest" (Isa 32:15).

We're facing an epidemic of spiritual and relational malnourishment, but as the Spirit seeps into our parched hearts, he springs forth with fruits of "love, joy, peace, patience, kindness, goodness, faithfulness, gentleness and self-control" (Gal 5:22–23). The One who fashioned miraculous life in a virgin's womb and partnered with the Messiah as promised throughout the Old Testament stands ready to blow a fresh wind upon us, to stir a renewed vigor for life more abundant (John 3:8).

I mentioned earlier that this final partnership brings the Spirit's story full circle. It reveals new layers of meaning to previously explored chapters and emphasizes a consistency in his character from Old Testament to New. Genesis opens with a scene of the Spirit drawing near the waters, hovering above the waves. At the close of Scripture, in the final chapters of Revelation, we find the imagery of water reflected in his invitation for us to draw near to him.

> "The Spirit and the bride say, 'Come!' And let the one who hears say, 'Come!' Let the one who is thirsty come; and let the one who wishes take the free gift of the water of life" (Rev 22:17).

From beginning to end, the Spirit's story is a story life. Mary responded to his invitation saying, "I am the Lord's servant. May your word to me be fulfilled" (Luke 1:38). And it was. Our response to his invitation will revolutionize our relationship with the whole of who God is. Our willingness to trust him opens the door for miraculous plot twists. This world overflows with illusions that promise life, but we must remember that there is only one source, one sustainer, one true spring of life. That's the Spirit Mary trusted. That's the Spirit the Messiah experienced. And that's the Spirit we are privileged to partner with, too.

So, come.

Drink deeply.

And live.

DIGGING DEEPER:

- How does this final partnership bring the Spirit's story full circle?

- How does the consistent portrayal of his character from Genesis to Revelation impact your connection with the Spirit?

- In what ways do you see the Spirit's heart reflected in Christ's actions as described in Isaiah 61:1?

- Following the introduction of this book you drew a "snapshot" of God the Father, God the Son, and God the Spirit. Visualize a new image of the Spirit now based on the characteristic you connected with most during this study.

- Did you find it easier this time? Why or why not?

- This chapter revealed the Spirit as the Spring of life. How does knowing this aspect of his personality encourage you to trust him more? And how might that trust transform your life?

Chapter Thirteen

The Epilogue

2 Corinthians 5:5–20

We've spent the previous twelve chapters exploring the Spirit's story through the eyes and experiences of Old Testament leaders, judges, prophets, and kings. His partnerships with real people facing real problems revealed who he is and why knowing him matters. Some of those people were born for the spotlight while others hid in a winepress or behind the luggage, but each one inspired us with a new aspects of the Spirit's unique personality. Those pieces came together in the greatest partnership of all between the Spirit and the long-awaited Messiah. Their collaboration unveiled the climax of God's redemptive narrative, but it was not the final curtain call.

The Spirit's story is not over.

We live in the epilogue. Christ accomplished our ultimate deliverance through his life, death, and resurrection, but today's faithful believers still await the full reality of that redemption. And while we wait in hopeful expectation, the Spirit partners with us.

> "And hope does not put us to shame, because God's love has been poured out into our hearts through the Holy Spirit, who has been given to us" (Rom 5:5).

We still wrestle with sin and temptations that can easily en-snare us, but we hold tight to the hope he offers for "where the Spirit of the Lord is, there is freedom" (2 Cor 3:17). Our world needs this freedom, and the Spirit partners with us as vessels of deliverance. He empowers each one of us to use our unique gifting for the good of all.

This quest began in hopes of connecting with the whole of who God is, Father, Son, *and* Spirit. I pray you've discovered a Spirit who is far more than the third wheel of the Trinity. He is transforming power. He is able to accomplish the impossible. He is the truth that guards and guides us. Like streams of water he seeps deep into our souls and brings forth fresh life.

Who he is matters in your story just as much as it did in the Old Testament tales we've explored. No-one is exempt from the unexpected scene changes that shift storylines in unwanted ways. Characters you planned to journey forward with may fall away. Forgotten chapters suddenly reopen while others falter before they're finished. Life is unpredictable. It rarely follows the script we anticipate, but a strong and steady relationship with the whole of who God is will see us through. The Spirit is key to that fullness of fellowship. The more we know him, the better we can trust him.

As your story moves forward, remember the trustworthy nature of the Spirit. When you encounter an unexpected opportu-nity to use your gifts for the good of God's kingdom, engage with the boldness of Bezalel who partnered with the Spirit to construct a house of worship and built a legacy that continues on to this very day. When exhaustion threatens to overwhelm you, rest in the Spirit's ability to cultivate community around you just like he did for Moses. When conflict disrupts life, find courage in the one Othniel encountered, the Champion of second chances who part-ners in relationship with the repentant to restore peace.

When you face a fork in the road and insecurities threaten to hold you back, reflect on Gideon's story, the weakest man of the weakest clan. The Spirit found him hiding in a winepress and shaped him into a hero who chose faith over fear time and time again. That same Spirit is able to transform your weaknesses into strengths, too. Let go of the way others see you, the way you see yourself, and trust the Author of impossible scripts to pen something purposeful with your life.

When you encounter the sting of rejection, remember Jephthah. Friends may hurt you. Family may fail you, but with the Spirit those places of wounding can become places of worship. When you wrestle with seasons of sin, learn from the mistakes of Samson and Saul. Flee temptation. Cling to the Hope of the fallen and repent like David. Face your failure, embrace forgiveness, and the Spirit will restore you.

When tragedy turns your world upside down, when mountains rise up unmovable before you, seek the Spirit Elijah encountered. Nothing is impossible for him. When darkness closes in and you can't find your way, listen to his voice. He is the one who spoke truth through the prophets to illuminate the paths of kings; He will guide you, too.

Above all, remember that the Spirit is the source and sustainer of life. Our true purpose finds fulfillment only in partnership with him. He helped create the world from nothing at the very beginning, and he continues making all things new even now.

> "The one who has fashioned us for this very purpose is God, who has given us the Spirit as a deposit, guaranteeing what is to come. Therefore, if anyone is in Christ, the new creation has come: The old has gone, the new is here! We are therefore Christ's ambassadors, as though God were making his appeal through us. Be reconciled to God" (2 Cor 5:5, 17, 20).

We are the encore to God's redemptive plan, his ambassadors in this world. We didn't earn such a privilege because we're perfect. Our calling comes by the grace of a Spirit willing to partner with us despite our imperfections.

Just as with each of the biblical characters we've explored, our resolve to trust him not only impacts our future but profits the entire kingdom community. The Spirit's heart beats in rhythm with relationship, and he invites his people into that perfect harmony, that fullness of fellowship. He is not separate from God the Father or Jesus Christ. They are one. Three in one. There may always be aspects of the Spirit's nature we can't fully comprehend this side of eternity, but Scripture consistently reveals his faithful character. He is a person we were always meant to know and trust. As we trust who he is, he will transform who we become and ignite fresh chapters of Spirit-fueled significance into the ever-changing story of our lives.

DIGGING DEEPER:

- Which Old Testament character did you most relate with? Why?

- What are three of the most impactful truths you discovered in this study?

- How can you demonstrate your belief in those truths by the way you live?

- Imagine what your life might look like if you wholeheartedly trusted the Spirit you've encountered in these pages. How does that differ from your present reality?

- What's holding you back from living that life right here, right now, just as you are?

- What aspect of the Spirit's unique personality can best encourage you to trust him and overcome the obstacle you identified above?

Appendix A

For Use in a Small Group or Sunday School

Story of the Spirit lends itself to an impactful group study by inspiring a shared adventure of knowing him better and trusting him more. It inspires authentic intimacy with biblical integrity, two essential components for every small group study! As your group navigates his role in the lives of real people throughout Scripture's narrative, you'll realize how understanding him revolutionizes your relationship with the whole of who God is.

Each chapter includes a set of questions for personal reflection and group discussion, but not every small group member is ready to reveal their innermost thoughts at the very beginning. The leader can initiate conversation for each week's assigned chapters with less invasive questions that relate to the material itself rather than personal application. For example, in chapter four you might ask, "What was significant about Othniel's name?" In chapter nine you could start with, "How did Saul and David first meet?" An introductory question for chapter eleven might be, "How would you summarize the first interaction between the prophet and king? The second? The third?"

Asking questions that already have answers identified in the book allows new or introverted members to engage in in the discussion without immediately divulging intimate details of their spiritual life. It also serves to refresh everyone's memory on the main story points for that week. If your group is comfortable diving straight into the personal application points, however, then follow their lead and dig right in!

Embrace the adventure as the Spirit infuses your community with a fresh sense of life and connectedness as you explore his story through Scripture together. We'd love to help you get the word out about your upcoming small group or Sunday school bible study! Please contact us at www.sarahjofairchild.com for digital media options including imagery for teaching presentations, social media posts, or promotional flyers.

Appendix B

For Use in a Sermon Series

Story of the Spirit lends itself to an impactful sermon series by inspiring your congregation to better understand who he is and how trusting him can revolutionize their life. It encourages authentic intimacy with biblical integrity, two essential components for every sermons series. The benefit of a book study like this is the way you can shape and mold the research within the chapters to create a truly unique series personalized for your people. You can assimilate the information into a sermon reflective of your style and relevant to your congregation's needs.

The chapters include relevant Scripture passages and follow the general outline included below. We hope you find it helpful as you tailoring your teaching to best fit the specific body of believers God has gathered at your church. The goal is not to communicate the author's agenda but reveal the biblical truths that inspire believers to know the Spirit better and trust him more.

GENERAL OUTLINE

- Introduction: Every teacher has their own manner of engaging the congregation's attention at the beginning of a sermon. Many use an illustration or analogy that relates to the material and answers the listener's unspoken question, "Why do I need to hear what they're about to say?"

- Tell the story: Introduce the Old Testament character. Provide necessary background information from Scripture, and then read the narrative of their story from the Bible using references provided within each chapter.

- Who he is: Connect the partnership between the Spirit and OT character to the personality trait of the Spirit it reveals. (Champion of second chances, Author of impossible scripts, etc.)

- Why he matters: Demonstrate how trusting the Spirit changed the storyline of that OT person—or how rejecting him impacted their life in cases like Samson and Saul. Illustrate how knowing and trusting this aspect of his character can transform our lives, too.

- Wrap it up: Invite your congregation to imagine what their life could look like if they trusted that aspect of the Spirit without reservation. You might encourage them to ponder what is preventing them from trusting him that way right now. Or you could encourage them to identify one action point they can do that week to start making that imagined potential a reality.

We'd love to help you get the word out about your upcoming small group or Sunday school bible study. Please contact us at www.sarahjofairchild.com for digital media options including imagery for teaching presentations, social media posts, or promotional flyers.

May the Spirit infuse your community with a fresh sense of life and connectedness as you explore his story through Scripture together!

Bibliography

Blomber, C.L. "Understanding." *International Standard Bible Encyclopedia.* Vol 4. Grand Rapids: William B Eerdmans, 1988.

Harrison, R. K. "Nazarite." *International Standard Bible Encyclopedia.* Vol 3. Grand Rapids: William B Eerdmans, 1986.

Henry, C.F.H. and R.K.H. "Knowledge." *International Standard Bible Encyclopedia.* Vol 3. Grand Rapids: William B Eerdmans, 1986.

Kaiser, Walter C. Jr. *The Expositor's Bible Commentary.* Vol 2. Grand Rapids: Zondervan, 1990.

Muller. "Wisdom." *TDOT.* Vol 4. Grand Rapids: William B Eerdmans, 1980.

Sheppard, G.T. "Wisdom." *International Standard Bible Encyclopedia.* Vol 4. Grand Rapids: William B Eerdmans, 1988.